GAIL DUFF
VEGETARIAN COOKERY

Happy Eating love Mum xxx 1988

Newman Turner

Produced by New Leaf Productions

Photography by Mick Duff
Design by Jim Wire
Series Editor: Elizabeth Gibson
Typeset by System Graphics Ltd., Folkestone

First published in 1985 by
The Hamlyn Publishing Group Limited
Bridge House, 69 London Road
Twickenham, Middlesex TW1 3SB England
Third impression 1987

Larsa D. L. TF. 690-1985

NOTE

1. Metric and imperial measurements have been
calculated separately. Use one set of measurements
only as they are not exact equivalents.

2. All spoon measures are level unless otherwise stated.

3. All recipes serve 4 unless otherwise stated.

4. Always set the oven at the temperature given.
Cooking times may vary according to the oven. For
fan-assisted ovens, times may be shorter, so always
follow manufacturers' instructions.

ACKNOWLEDGEMENTS
We would like to thank: Valerie Clarke, Caroline
Ward, Caroline Owens, Billie Wray and Bill Wood.
Also: Honesty Wholefoods, Union St., Maidstone,
Kent, Brian Cook and Son, Charing, Kent,
Lurcocks of Lenham, Kent, and Nasons of
Canterbury, Kent.

YOU'RE HOT STUFF, MUM!

Main picture by Miki Moulton/Inset by Francis Coney

'My mother is the sweetest person in the world and a fantastic cook,' says TV-am newsreader Lisa Aziz. 'I would travel miles to eat her food — it's perfection.

Lisa's mother Anne is English and her father Suhail is Bangladeshi. Anne was always a great cook and Suhail taught her to make curries — he now admits hers are better than his.

'My favourite is Mum's egg, potato and cauliflower curry,' says Lisa, 'and I still rush home for it. She does a great coconut rice with it — you'd never get the like in a restaurant.

'I've always been spoilt as far as catering arrangements are concerned. My parents even arrive with dishes of food when they come to visit. I got married recently to Frank, a Dutchman, a race not usually rated as brilliant cooks. What happens? He won't allow me in the kitchen! How could I be so lucky?

'I'm grateful that I've been so well looked after. Mum is a unique lady with a full-time job. But she still has the energy and enthusiasm to keep us supplied with her wonderful food!' **TVT**

MUM'S CURRY

Simple curry made from store cupboard ingredients.
Serves 4
2tbsp oil
1 large onion, chopped
2 cloves garlic, crushed
1tsp chilli powder
2tsp turmeric
2tsp garam masala
2tsp ground coriander
1tsp garlic powder
2 large potatoes, peeled and chunked
1 small cauliflower in florets
1pt/600ml vegetable stock
salt and pepper
8 hard-boiled eggs, shelled

Heat oil in pan, fry onion and garlic until soft. Stir in spices and cook for further minute, stirring. Add potatoes, cauliflower and vegetable stock. Season with salt and pepper. Cover and cook for 10min. Slit eggs lengthwise, add to pan. Simmer for a further 6min. Add coriander.
Time to prepare: 10min
Time to cook: 25min
Calories: 180 without rice and salad

MUM'S RICE

Subtly flavoured rice dish with shreds of fresh coconut. A perfect accompaniment to curry.
Serves 4
2tbsp oil
1 clove garlic, crushed
8oz/225g long grain rice
½pint/300ml coconut milk
salt and freshly ground black pepper
3tbsp fresh coconut, grated
2tbsp frozen peas, defrosted
1 hard-boiled egg, peeled and sliced

Heat oil in a pan and fry garlic for 1min. Add rice and stir to coat in oily mixture. Pour over coconut milk and top up with enough water to just cover. Bring to the boil, cover and simmer until rice is tender and all liquid is absorbed. Add a little more water if necessary. Season. Stir in grated coconut and peas and season again. Pile into a serving bowl and decorate with hard-boiled egg slices.
Time to prepare: 5min
Time to cook: 25min
Calories: 150

MUM'S SALAD

Lettuce, tomato, cucumber and onion in spicy mint dressing.
Serves 4
1 iceberg lettuce, rinsed
1 onion, peeled and finely sliced
4 tomatoes, wiped and quartered
1 cucumber, wiped and sliced

For the dressing:
6tbsp sunflower oil
2tbsp white wine vinegar
1tsp mustard
1tsp paprika
1tbsp fresh mint, chopped
salt and pepper
pinch of sugar

Drain lettuce and pat dry. Shred finely and place in a bowl. Add onion, tomatoes and cucumber and toss to mix. Shake dressing ingredients in a screw-top jar and drizzle over salad. Toss again to coat and arrange on 4 small serving plates. Serve with egg, potato and cauliflower curry and coconut rice.
Time to prepare: 10min
Time to cook: None
Calories: 85

...few days in one of the world... most exciting cities, staying at the wonderful five-star Waldorf Astoria, one of the Big Apple's best hotels.

They will be taken on an exclusive helicopter tour of the city's skyline and have the chance to visit a Broadway show. There will also be plenty of time to do last-minute Christmas shopping before a really smooth flight back to the UK on Christmas Eve on the fabulous Concorde.

This is the sort of romantic trip that might have even rekindled the flames of romance lost by the warring couple in CBS/Fox's latest release, *The War of the Roses*, which stars Danny DeVito as a divorce lawyer recounting the story of how Oliver and Barbara — played by Michael Douglas and Kathleen Turner — grow to hate each other.

It's a black comedy with definitely more than it's fair share of laughs, with terrific performances from all the leading actors.

Fifty runners-up will each receive a copy of the movie, plus a stunning flower display by London's leading florist, Terry Chivers, sent by Interflora to someone they love. **TVT**

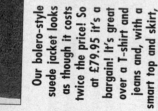

Our bolero-style suede jacket looks as though it costs twice the price! So at £79.95 it's a bargain! It's great over a T-shirt and jeans and, with a smart top and skirt, it's perfect for a dressy occasion

...y happiness.

Born in Poland, Joanna came to England on holiday eight years ago, fell in love with it, found success as an actress and stayed.

Joanna's stunning good looks make her the ideal model for our suede jacket — this week's special fashion offer.

Made in England to an extremely high standard, this genuine suede jacket is ideal for both casual and evening wear — as our pictures show.

Available in chestnut brown (A) or midnight black (B), the jackets come in sizes 10-18 (length approximately 18in from nape of neck to hem).

Our price to you is an unbelievable £79.95 (including p&p and VAT). You won't find a jacket of this quality at such a low price elsewhere.

To order, simply fill in the coupon indicating colour, size and number required and send it, together with your cheque or postal orders, crossed and made payable to Independent Television Publications Ltd, to: TVTimes Suede Jacket Offer, PO Box 6, Kettering, Northants NN15 5JW.

Access and Visa card holders may also place their order by telephoning Kettering (0536) 726681.

If you should be in any way dissatisfied please return the goods within seven days, using Royal Mail compensation parcel post, to the address stated above and a full refund or replacement will be sent to you. **TVT**

To: *TVTimes* Suede Jacket Offer,
PO Box 6, Kettering, Northants NN15 5JW,
Please indicate colour (write A in the appropriate box if you want chestnut brown, B for midnight black), size and number required. Price includes postage and VAT. Please allow 28 days for delivery from receipt of order. Offer closes 31 December 1990 subject to availability.

ITEM	SIZE	COLOUR	NO REQ	COST
Jacket @ £79.95				
				TOTAL

BLOCK LETTERS, PLEASE

I enclose cheque/POs No .... Value £. ....
Debit my Access/Visa card (delete where not applicable)
Account No ....
Signature ....
Name ....
Address ....
.... Postcode ....

94

CONTENTS

Introduction   4
   Why Eat Vegetarian Food?
   How to Eat Vegetarian Food
   Types of Vegetarianism
   Protein Foods
Soups & Starters   6
Main Dishes   14
Light Meals & Snacks   26
Salads, Dressings & Vegetables   34
Grain Accompaniments   40
Baking   46
Desserts   54
Two Special Menus   60
Index   64

INTRODUCTION

Meat-free eating is becoming increasingly popular as more and more people realise how varied, appetising and healthy a vegetarian diet can be. Some have chosen to give up meat and fish altogether; others have found it better to integrate vegetarian meals with meat ones. Whichever way we choose, we find that vegetarian meals add an entirely new aspect to our diet.

Why Eat Vegetarian food?

Some people, concerned about techniques of factory farming, are turning to vegetarian food on purely moral grounds. Probably the main reason, however, is the current awareness that food affects our health.

Books and doctors tell us that we should be eating less fat, salt, and sugar and more fibre. A wholefood vegetarian diet can help us to achieve these aims. With no meat in the diet and more of such vegetable protein foods as pulses and nuts, we automatically cut down on saturated animal fats. We still include cheese and eggs, but very often they are added to a mixture of other low fat, high fibre ingredients; rarely do we eat them in too great a quantity. Many vegetarians also give up buying baked products such as pies, which also contain saturated fats; they frequently substitute vegetable oils in place of butter for cooking.

If you cook vegetarian food well, with plenty of cleverly used herbs and spices for flavour, you find that only a few dishes need salt for flavouring. Taste the dish when you have completed it and only add salt if you think it absolutely necessary. Salt is necessary for successful bread making, and it gives pasta and plainly boiled rice a better flavour; but even so, there is no need to add too much.

Because sugar is not an animal product, giving it up is not, in theory, essential to a vegetarian diet; however, you should use it only in moderation. Most vegetarians prefer to make as much of their own food as possible and as a result are not eating the hidden sugar that is in so many commercial products from baked beans to so-called savoury biscuits. But if you must buy prepared food, look in health shops to find products such as sugar-free jam and tomato ketchup that will help you avoid it.

And what about fibre? A healthy vegetarian diet includes nuts and pulses, plenty of fresh fruits and vegetables and—most importantly—whole grains such as wholewheat bread or brown rice. If you eat a

variety of all these products you need never worry about whether you are getting enough fibre.

A vegetarian diet also contributes to good health because it includes a wide range of ingredients. Each type of food contains different vitamins and minerals in varying proportions, providing your body with a little of everything it needs rather than too much of one type of nutrient.

Yet another advantage of vegetarian cookery is the matter of economy. Meals made with pulses, grains, nuts, cheese and eggs tend to be cheaper than many based on meat and fish. They are therefore a boon to the budgeting housewife, whether she chooses to serve them all the time or several times a week.

Lastly there is the question of enjoyment. Because you will be using fresh, natural ingredients, you will find the flavour of whatever you make superb: from the simple salads and plain brown rice to the more complicated main meals. If you have ever eaten meals based only on the "meat-and-two-veg" theme, you will find that vegetarian ingredients and mixed main meals adds variety to your daily menus. A whole range of new foods can be added to the old favourites in your store-cupboard, and your palate will be tempted by new and delicious flavours and textures.

How to Eat Vegetarian food

Vegetarian cookery is not just for vegetarians. Everybody can enjoy it. If you have always been a meat eater, there is no reason, provided you are in sound health, that you should not improve diet and health further by gradually introducing vegetarian meals into your weekly menus. A good balance would be meat or fish meals for four or perhaps only three days a week, with vegetarian meals in between.

In many of the following recipes such as the soups and first courses, the vegetable or grain accompaniments can be served as part of a meal which includes meat as a main course. The snacks and light meals can be served for lunch or supper on the same day.

Even if you would like to become completely vegetarian, follow the same "easy-does-it" rule; otherwise you may find the sudden change too much of a shock to your system. Begin by making sure that every ingredient you use is wholefood. That is, always use wholewheat flour, bread and pasta, other whole grains such as brown rice, plenty of fresh fruits and vegetables, little sugar, and no processed foods. The next step is to eat meat only once a day and after that, gradually replace meat meals with vegetarian ones. That way, your digestive system will find the new food easier to absorb; meanwhile you will gradually come to enjoy all the new flavours, textures and cooking methods.

Types of Vegetarianism

Most vegetarians are content simply to give up meat and fish and still continue to eat eggs or dairy products—or both. Those who eat dairy products but not eggs are technically referred to as *lacto-vegetarians*. If you eat both, the term is *lacto-ovo-vegetarian*.

If for health reasons—some people are allergic to eggs or dairy products—or for moral reasons you give up these products as well as meat and fish, you then become a *vegan* who relies on nuts, grains, pulses and soya bean products for protein. As this book is intended to be a basic introduction to vegetarian food, it does not cater for vegans—although many of the recipes would be suitable for a vegan diet.

Protein Foods

The main protein foods used in this book are eggs, cheese, nuts and pulses, all of which are familiar ingredients whether or not you are already a vegetarian, and all of which are easily obtainable in supermarkets and health food shops.

Eggs and cheese are animal products and are called *first-class protein foods*. This means that they contain the type of protein that can immediately be used by the body for growth and repair of tissues. They do not have to be combined with any other ingredients.

Pulses and nuts are called *second-class protein foods*. In order to supply your body with usable protein, they must be eaten in the same meal with wholegrain products such a wholewheat bread or pasta, brown rice, or one of the other more unusual grains. (See page 40.) You will find that the flavours and textures blend extremely well; there are many combinations of ingredients with which to experiment.

SOUPS & STARTERS

A vegetarian soup or first course can be served before any meal. Many soups, in fact, are made of purely vegetarian ingredients; probably the only difference that you will discover when making up the following recipes is that you will be using a vegetable stock rather than one based on chicken or beef. Many health food shops sell vegetable stock cubes; however, as with meat stocks, you will achieve a better flavour if you make your own.

Small portions of vegetables, either cooked or served as a small salad, make ideal starters, particularly if they are cleverly combined with fruits, nuts or cheese.

Choose your vegetables well, make them look attractive, and you will set the scene for a memorable meal that should please everybody.

BASIC VEGETABLE STOCK

1 large onion, quartered, not peeled
2 celery sticks, broken in several pieces
2 carrots, split lengthways
1 small potato, halved, not peeled
several outer leaves of cabbage or spring greens
bouquet garni
1 teaspoon black peppercorns
1 teaspoon vegetable concentrate such as Vecon
3.5 litres/6 pints water

Put all the ingredients into a large saucepan. Bring them to the boil. Simmer, uncovered, for 1 hour.

Cool the stock and strain it. Put it into a covered plastic container and store in the refrigerator. It will keep for up to 1 week.

GRATED CARROT SOUP

450g/1lb carrots
25g/1oz butter
1 large onion, finely chopped
1 clove garlic, finely chopped
1 teaspoon ground cumin
1 teaspoon ground coriander
900ml/1½ pints Basic vegetable stock (p.6)
bouquet garni
150ml/¼ pint yoghurt

Coarsely grate the carrots. Melt the butter in a saucepan over a low heat. Mix in the carrots, onion, garlic and spices. Cover and cook them gently for 10 minutes. Pour in the stock and bring to the boil. Add the bouquet garni and simmer, covered, for 20 minutes.

Take the soup from the heat and remove the bouquet garni. Stir in the yoghurt just before serving.

SIMPLE CAULIFLOWER SOUP WITH CHEESE

1 large cauliflower
1 large onion
900ml/1½ pints, Basic vegetable stock (p.6)
sea salt and freshly ground black pepper
bouquet garni
100g/4oz Cheddar cheese, grated

Finely chop the cauliflower and the onion. Put them into a saucepan with the stock. Season and add the bouquet garni. Bring them to the boil, cover and simmer for 20 minutes. Remove the bouquet garni and either work the soup in a blender or food processor or rub it through the fine blade of a vegetable mill.

Return the soup to the saucepan and reheat. Put a portion of the cheese in the bottom of each of four soup bowls. Pour in the soup and stir it round so that the cheese melts in swirls.

CURRIED CELERY AND APPLE SOUP

4 large celery sticks
1 large cooking apple
100g/4oz potatoes
1 medium onion
25g/1oz butter
1 tablespoon curry powder
900ml/1½ pints Basic vegetable stock (p.6)
2 tablespoons chopped celery leaves

Chop the celery. Peel, quarter, core and slice the apple. Peel and thinly slice the potatoes. Thinly slice the onion.

Melt the butter in a saucepan over a low heat. Stir in the celery, apple, potatoes, onion and curry powder. Cover them and cook them gently for 10 minutes. Pour in the stock and bring it to the boil. Cover and simmer for 20 minutes. Cool the soup a little and either work it in a blender or food processor until it is smooth or put it through the fine blade of a vegetable mill.

Return the soup to the saucepan and reheat. Serve garnished with the celery leaves.

LEEK, CARROT AND POTATO SOUP

225g/8oz leeks
225g/8oz carrots
225g/8oz potatoes
25g/1oz vegetable margarine or butter
900ml/1½ pints Basic vegetable stock (p.6)
bouquet garni
freshly ground black pepper
8 sage leaves, finely chopped
2 tablespoons flaked almonds, toasted (optional)

Thinly slice the leeks and carrots. Peel and thinly slice the potatoes. Melt the margarine or butter in a saucepan over a low heat. Stir in the vegetables; cover them and cook them gently for 10 minutes.

Pour in the stock and bring it to the boil. Add the bouquet garni and season with the pepper. Cover and simmer for 20 minutes.

Remove pan from heat. Remove the bouquet garni. Either put the soup through the fine blade of a vegetable mill or work it in a blender or food processor until it is smooth. Return the soup to the pan and add the sage. Reheat the soup and pour it into individual bowls. Scatter the toasted almonds over the top if desired.

ONION, MUSHROOM AND GREEN PEPPER SOUP

1 large onion
175g/6oz dark, flat mushrooms
1 large green pepper
4 tablespoons oil
1 clove garlic, finely chopped
1 tablespoon wholewheat flour
900ml/1½ pints Basic vegetable stock (p.6)
2 tablespoons chopped marjoram
   (or 1 tablespoon dried)

Finely chop the onion, mushrooms and pepper. Heat the oil in a saucepan over a low heat. Stir in the prepared vegetables plus the garlic. Cover and cook them gently for 10 minutes.

Stir in the flour and stock. Bring them to the boil, stirring. Add the marjoram and simmer, uncovered, for 15 minutes.

SIMPLE TOMATO SOUP

675g/1½lb ripe tomatoes
25g/1oz vegetable margarine or butter
1 large onion, finely chopped
600ml/1 pint Basic vegetable stock (p.6)
4 tablespoons chopped fresh mixed herbs
   (or 1½ tablespoons dried)
4 tablespoons soured cream

Scald, peel and chop the tomatoes. Melt the butter in a saucepan on a low heat. Put in the onion; cover and cook gently for 5 minutes. Put in the tomatoes; cover and cook for 5 minutes. Mash the tomatoes to a purée using a potato masher or fish slice. Pour in the stock and bring it to the boil. Add the herbs. Cover and simmer for 15 minutes.

Pour the soup into individual bowls and float 1 tablespoon soured cream on the top of each one.

GRILLED AUBERGINES WITH SESAME SEEDS

450g/1lb aubergines
2 tablespoons sea salt
2 tomatoes
125/ml/4 fl oz olive oil
juice of 1 lemon
2 tablespoons tomato purée
1 clove garlic, crushed
1 teaspoon paprika
pinch of cayenne
3 tablespoons sesame seeds
4 small parsley sprigs

Cut the aubergines into 1-cm/⅜-in slices. Layer them in a colander with salt and leave them to drain for 30 minutes. Rinse them under cold water and dry them with kitchen paper.

Cut the tomatoes into jagged-edged halves. Beat the oil, lemon juice, tomato purée, garlic, paprika and cayenne together.

Heat the grill to high. Lay as many aubergine slices as you can on the rack and brush the uppermost sides with the dressing. Grill them for 2 minutes; turn them over and brush them again. Scatter some sesame seeds over the top and grill them for a further 2 minutes. Remove them to keep them warm. Grill the rest in the same way.

Scatter the tomatoes with sesame seeds and grill them, cut side up, for 2 minutes only.

Divide the aubergine slices and tomato halves between four individual plates.

TOMATOES FULL OF CAMEMBERT

4 large tomatoes, or 8 small
100g/4oz Camembert
2 tablespoons chopped parsley
2 tablespoons wholewheat breadcrumbs, browned
8 small squares wholewheat toast
8 small parsley sprigs

Heat the oven to 170°C/325°F/Gas 3. Cut the tomatoes in half crossways; scoop out and discard the centres. (They can be reserved for soup if wished.) Finely dice the Camembert.

Put half the cheese into the tomatoes. Sprinkle in the parsley and then put in the remaining cheese.

Put the tomatoes into a lightly greased, ovenproof dish. Cover them with foil and put them into the oven for 15 minutes. Remove the foil. Sprinkle them with the crumbs and return them to the oven for a further 5 minutes.

Serve each tomato half on a small square of toast garnished with a parsley sprig.

HOT CELERY AND WALNUT SALAD

4 large celery sticks
2 medium cooking apples or 1 really large
3 tablespoons oil
1 clove garlic, finely chopped
100g/4oz walnuts, chopped
50g/2oz raisins
2 tablespoons vinegar

Dice the celery. Quarter, core and slice the apples.

Heat the oil in a frying pan over a moderate heat. Put in the celery and garlic and stir them for 2 minutes. Put in the walnuts, raisins and apples and cook for 1 minute more. Pour in the vinegar and let it bubble.

Divide the salad between four small bowls.

AVOCADO WITH GREEN PEPPER CHEESE

2 ripe avocados
1 medium-sized green pepper
125ml/4oz curd cheese
1 tablespoon tomato purée
pinch of cayenne

Halve and stone the avocados. Core, deseed and very finely chop the pepper. Put the cheese into a bowl and beat in the tomato purée and cayenne. Fold in the green pepper.

Pile the mixture into the avocado halves.

CARROT AND BANANA SALAD

350g/12oz carrots
2 ripe bananas
4 tablespoons cider vinegar
2 tablespoons poppy seeds
50g/2oz peanuts
1 small cucumber

Finely grate the carrots. Mash the bananas and mix in the vinegar to make a thick dressing. Add the carrots, poppy seeds and peanuts and mix well. Thinly slice the cucumber.

Arrange a portion of the carrot salad in the centre of each of four small plates. Put cucumber rings round the edge and a small piece of cucumber on top as a garnish.

CHICORY, GRAPE AND ORANGE SALAD

2 heads chicory
175g/6oz black grapes
2 medium oranges
juice of 1 lemon
1 teaspoon honey
4 tablepoons natural yoghurt
1 tablespoon Tahini
1 clove garlic, crushed with a pinch of sea salt
freshly ground black pepper

Trim the stem ends from the chicory. Cut each head in half lengthways and thinly slice it. Halve and seed the grapes. Cut the rind and pith from the oranges. Cut each one in half lengthways and each half into four slices. Beat together the remaining ingredients.

Put a portion of chicory in the centre of each of four small plates. Spoon the dressing over the top. Put black grape halves and orange slices around the edge and garnish the top with more grape halves.

MAIN DISHES

Vegetarian main meals are generally more interesting both to prepare and to eat than those based on meat or fish because they are often made up of combinations of two or more protein ingredients which give delicious contrasts of colour, texture and flavour.

Where pulses and nuts are used, if no grain product is used in the main dish itself, find an accompanying grain dish (see pages 40–47) to go with it.

If you are cooking pulses, follow these basic instructions. There are two ways of soaking them: 1. Soak them overnight, then bring them to the boil; boil them rapidly for 10 minutes and then drain them. 2. Put them into a saucepan with cold water and bring them to the boil. Boil them rapidly for 10 minutes; take the pan from the heat; leave the beans in the water for 2 hours and drain them. The 10-minute boiling in each of the methods will ensure that any substances which may cause mild stomach upsets will be destroyed.

After draining the beans, put them into a saucepan with fresh water and cook them gently until they are soft, or for as long as a recipe requires. In order to be completely cooked, *aduki beans* and *mung beans* need 40–45 minutes; *black-eyed beans* 50 minutes–1 hour; *haricot beans, pinto beans/flageolet,* and all *kidney beans* 1½ hours; *butter beans* 1½–2 hours; and *chickpeas* 2–2½ hours.

TWO-BEAN SIMMER POT

100g/4oz red kidney beans
100g/4oz haricot beans
1 red pepper
1 green pepper
4 large celery sticks
225/8oz tomatoes
1 large onion
3 tablespoons sunflower oil
1 clove garlic, finely chopped
1 teaspoon paprika
150ml/¼ pint tomato-and-vegetable juice★

Soak and cook both types of beans separately. (See this page.) Core and deseed the peppers and cut them into 2-cm/¾-inch squares. Cut the celery into pieces the same size. Scald, peel and chop the tomatoes. Finely chop the onion.

Heat the oil in a saucepan on a low heat. Put in the onion, garlic, peppers and celery. Cover them and cook them for 10 minutes. Stir in the beans and paprika. Pour in the tomato-and-vegetable juice and bring it to the boil. Cover and simmer for 15 minutes. Add the tomatoes; cover again and cook for a further 2 minutes.
★*Tomato-and-vegetable juice* can be bought in 300ml/11 fl oz cans under the brand name V8.

PINTO BEANS WITH MILLET AND CHEESE

225g/8oz pinto beans
3 tablespoons oil
1 large onion, finely chopped
1 clove garlic, finely chopped
1 teaspoon paprika
¼ teaspoon cayenne
225g/8oz millet
300ml/½ pint tomato juice
300ml/½ pint Basic vegetable stock (p.6)
450g/1lb tomatoes
100g/4oz Cheddar cheese, grated

Put the beans into a saucepan and cover them with water. Bring them to the boil. Boil them rapidly for 10 minutes. Take the pan from the heat and leave the beans to soak in the water for 2 hours. Drain the beans and put them into a saucepan of fresh water. Bring them to the boil. Cover and simmer them for 1½ hours or until they are soft. Drain them.

Heat the oil in a saucepan on a low heat. Put in the onion and garlic and soften them. Mix in the paprika, cayenne and millet. Stir on the heat for 1 minute. Pour in the tomato juice and stock and bring them to the boil. Put in the beans. Cover and simmer for 20 minutes or until the millet is soft and fluffy.

While the millet is cooking, chop the tomatoes. They can be scalded and peeled first if wished, but this is not essential.

When the millet is done, mix in the cheese and tomatoes.

SPICED BLACK-EYED BEAN AND RICE SOUP

225g/8oz black-eyed beans
one 400-g/14-ox tin tomatoes in juice
2 tablespoons oil
1 large onion, finely chopped
1 clove garlic, finely chopped
100g/4oz long-grain brown rice
1 teaspoon paprika
1 teaspoon cinnamon
pinch of cayenne
900ml/1½ pints Basic vegetable stock (p.6)
50g/2oz grated Cheddar cheese, optional

Put the beans into a saucepan and cover them with water. Bring them to the boil. Boil them rapidly for 10 minutes. Take the pan from the heat and leave the beans to soak in the water for 2 hours. Drain the beans and put them into a saucepan of fresh water. Bring them to the boil. Cover and simmer them for 30 minutes. Drain them.

Liquidise the tomatoes with their juice. Heat the oil in a saucepan on a low heat. Put in the onion and soften it. Stir in the rice and spices and cook, stirring, for 2 minutes.

Pour in the tomatoes and stock. Bring them to the boil. Put in the beans. Cover and simmer for 45 minutes or until the rice and beans are soft.

Serve topped with the grated cheese if wished.

Accompany the soup with wholewheat bread and follow it with a salad.

CHICKPEA, CELERY AND APPLE SALAD

225g/8oz chickpeas
6 large celery sticks
2 dessert apples
6 tablespoons soured cream
3 tablespoons cider vinegar
½ teaspoon mustard powder
1 clove garlic, crushed

Put the chickpeas into a saucepan and cover them with water. Bring them to the boil and boil them rapidly for 10 minutes. Take the pan from the heat and leave the chickpeas to soak for 2 hours. Drain them. Return them to the saucepan with fresh water. Bring them to the boil and simmer for 2½–3 hours or until they are soft. Drain and cool them.

Thinly slice the celery sticks. Core and chop the apples. Mix them into the chickpeas.

Beat the remaining ingredients together to make the dressing. Fold them into the salad.

Serve with lettuce, tomatoes and cucumber plus a potato or rice salad.

BROWN LENTILS WITH PARSLEY AND WATERCRESS

3 tablespoons oil
1 large onion, finely chopped
225g/8oz small brown (Chinese) lentils
600ml/1 pint Basic vegetable stock (p.6)
2 tablespoons Worcestershire sauce
4 tablespoons chopped parsley
50g/2oz watercress, finely chopped

Heat the oil in a saucepan on a low heat. Put in the onion and soften it. Add the lentils and stir on the heat for half a minute.

Pour in the stock and bring it to the boil. Add the Worcestershire sauce, parsley and watercress. Cover and cook gently for 50 minutes or until the lentils are soft and most of the stock has been absorbed.

GREEN LENTIL RATATOUILLE

225g/8oz aubergines
2 green peppers
1 red pepper
1 large onion
4 tablespoons sunflower oil
1 clove garlic, finely chopped
225g/8oz green lentils
1 teaspoon paprika
¼ teaspoon cayenne
300ml/½ pint Basic vegetable stock (p.6)
300ml/½ pint tomato juice OR tomato-and-vegetable juice (p.14)
1 bay leaf

Cut the aubergines into 2-cm/¾-in dice. Put them into a colander and sprinkle them with the salt. Leave them to drain for 20 minutes. Run cold water through them and dry them with kitchen paper. Core and deseed the peppers and cut them into 2-cm/¾-in dice. Finely chop the onion.

Heat the oil in a flameproof casserole or large saucepan over a low heat. Put in the onion and garlic and soften them. Mix in the peppers and aubergine. Cover and cook for 5 minutes. Stir in the lentils, paprika and cayenne and cook them for 1 minute, stirring. Pour in the stock and tomato juice and bring them to the boil. Add the bayleaf. Simmer, covered, for 45 minutes.

HEARTY CABBAGE OMELETTE

350g/12oz green cabbage
3 celery sticks
2 tablespoons oil
150ml/¼ pint milk
½ teaspoon dried mixed herbs
6 eggs
2 tablespoons tomato purée
50g/2oz fresh wholewheat breadcrumbs

Shred the cabbage and finely chop the celery. Heat the oil in a 25-cm/10-in frying pan on a high heat. Put in the cabbage and celery and stir them on the heat for 1 minute. Pour in the milk and bring it to the boil. Add the herbs. Cover and cook on a low to medium heat for 15 minutes, stirring twice. The cabbage should be just tender.

While the cabbage is cooking beat the eggs with the tomato purée and stir in the breadcrumbs. Heat the grill to high.

Pour the egg mixture into the pan and cook on a low heat until it begins to set. Transfer the pan to the grill and cook the omelette until it is set and the top is golden. Serve straight from the pan.

LEEK AND BEAN MACARONI

225g/8oz flageolets or haricot beans
225g/8oz wholewheat macaroni
350g/12oz leeks
2 tablespoons oil
2 teaspoons spiced coarse-grain mustard
25g/1oz butter
3 tablespoons wholewheat flour
450ml/¾ pint milk
100g/4oz Wensleydale cheese, grated

Put the beans into a saucepan and cover them with cold water. Bring them to the boil and boil them rapidly for 10 minutes. Take the pan from the heat and leave them to soak for 2 hours. Drain them. Return them to the saucepan with fresh water. Bring them to the boil. Cover and simmer them for 1 hour 20 minutes or until they are tender. Drain them.

Cook the macaroni in lightly salted water for 15 minutes or until tender. Drain it.

Wash and thinly slice the leeks. Heat the oil in a large frying pan on a high heat. Put in the leeks and stir-fry them for 4 minutes. Take the pan from the heat. Mix in the mustard and the beans.

Heat the oven to 200°C/400°F/Gas 6. Melt the butter in a saucepan over a medium heat. Stir in the flour and the milk. Bring the sauce to the boil, stirring. Simmer it for 2 minutes. Take the pan from the heat and beat in about two-thirds of the cheese.

Put one-third of the macaroni into the bottom of a deep, ovenproof dish. Cover it with one-third of the sauce and then half the leek and bean mixture. Put in another third each of the macaroni and the sauce, then all the remaining leeks. Then the remaining third of the macaroni and the sauce. Scatter the remaining cheese over the top.

Put the dish into the oven for 20 minutes or until the top is beginning to brown.

CURRIED WHEAT AND LENTIL LOAF

225g/8oz split red lentils
2 tablespoons oil
1 large onion, finely chopped
1 clove garlic, finely chopped
2 teaspoons hot Madras curry powder
750ml/1¼ pints Basic vegetable stock or water (p.6)
2 bay leaves
225g/8oz burghul wheat (see p.40)
150ml/¼ pint natural yoghurt
oil for greasing

Sauce
150ml/¼ pint natural yoghurt
¼ teaspoon curry paste
½ medium cucumber, finely chopped

Heat the oil in a saucepan on a low heat. Put in the onion and garlic and soften them. Stir in the lentils and curry powder. Cook them for 1 minute. Pour in the stock or water and bring it to the boil. Cover and simmer for 40 minutes or until the lentils are soft but there is still enough liquid to make the consistency of a very thick soup. Remove pan from heat.

While the lentils are cooking, soak the wheat in warm water for 20 minutes. Drain it and squeeze it dry. Heat the oven to 190°C/375°F/Gas 5.

Mix half the lentils and all the yoghurt into the wheat. Put half this mixture in an even layer in a 20-cm/8-in diameter cake tin. Put in the remaining lentils and top them with the remaining wheat mixture.

Bake the cake for 25 minutes or until the top is browned. Turn it onto a serving plate and serve the sauce separately.

To make the sauce, beat the yoghurt with the curry paste. Mix in the cucumber. Serve over the loaf.

AVOCADO OMELETTE

1 large, ripe avocado
4 tablespoons oil
1 medium onion, finely chopped
1 clove garlic, finely chopped
1 medium-sized green pepper, cored, deseeded
    and chopped
6 eggs
1 tablespoon tomato purée
½ teaspoon Tabasco sauce
1 teaspoon paprika
2 tablespoons chopped parsley

Peel and stone the avocado and cut it into thin slices about 5cm/2in long. Heat the oil in an omelette pan on a low heat. Mix in the onion, garlic and pepper and cook them until the onion is soft.

Beat the eggs with the tomato purée, Tabasco, paprika and parsley. Put the slices of avocado into the pan and distribute them evenly. Heat the grill to high.

Pour the egg mixture into the pan and cook it, tipping the pan and lifting the sides of the omelette to let as much of the mixture as possible get to the sides and bottom of the pan.

When the underside of the omelette is brown, transfer the pan to the grill. Cook until the omelette is golden brown and risen. Cut into four and serve straight from the pan.

PASTA AND SPINACH SCRAMBLE

225g/8oz wholewheat pasta spirals or rings
350g/12oz spinach
225g/8oz tomatoes
6 eggs, beaten
75g/3oz Cheddar cheese, grated
50g/2oz butter

Cook the pasta in lightly salted water for 15 minutes or until tender. Drain it; run cold water through it and drain it again.

Break off the stems of the spinach at the point where they meet the leaves. Finely chop the leaves. Scald, peel and chop the tomatoes. Beat the eggs with the cheese.

Melt 25g/1oz of the butter in a saucepan on a low heat. Add the tomatoes and cook them for 1 minute. Stir in the egg mixture and continue stirring until it is just beginning to set. Take the pan from the heat.

Melt the remaining butter in a paella pan or a wok on a high heat. Put in the spinach and stir it until it has wilted and softened, about 5 minutes. Put in the egg mixture and the pasta and stir to heat through.

LEEK ROULADE

225g/8oz leeks
4 eggs, separated
2 tablespoons grated Parmesan cheese
2 tablespoons chopped parsley
2 eggs, hard–boiled
75g/3oz mushrooms
15g/½oz vegetable margarine or butter
1 tablespoon wholewheat flour
150ml/¼ pint milk
1 teaspoon spiced coarse-grain mustard

Heat the oven to 200°C/400°F/Gas 6. Line a swiss roll tin with greased greaseproof paper.

Wash and thinly slice the leeks. Bring a pan of water to the boil. Put in the leeks and cook them for 3 minutes. Drain them and run cold water through them. Drain again.

Beat the egg yolks. Mix in 1 tablespoon of the cheese, the leeks and the parsley. Stiffly whisk the egg whites. Fold them into the yolk mixture. Spread the mixture evenly over the paper in the tin. Bake it for 15 minutes or until it is firm but not coloured.

While the roulade is cooking, chop the eggs and the mushrooms. Melt the margarine or butter in a saucepan on a low heat. Put in the mushrooms and cook them for 2 minutes. Stir in the flour and milk and bring them to the boil, stirring. Simmer the sauce for 2 minutes. Take the pan from the heat. Beat in the mustard and mix in the eggs.

When the roulade is cooked, spread the sauce and eggs evenly over the top. Lift one short end of the greaseproof paper and carefully roll up the roulade. Ease it from the paper onto a heatproof plate. Scatter the remaining Parmesan cheese over the top.

Put the roulade under a high grill to lightly brown the cheese.

CURRIED SAVOY WITH CASHEWS AND EGGS

6 eggs
1 large savoy cabbage
3 tablespoons oil
1 large onion, thinly sliced
1 clove garlic, finely chopped
15g/3oz cashew nuts
2 teaspoons curry powder
½ teaspoon ground cumin
½ teaspoon ground coriander
125ml/4 fl oz Basic vegetable stock (p. 6)
juice of ½ lemon
5 tablespoons natural yoghurt

Hard boil and chop the eggs. Finely shred the cabbage.

Heat the oil in a large saucepan on a low heat. Put in the onion and garlic and soften them. Stir in the

Pour in the cider and bring it to the boil. Add the crushed peppercorns and juniper berries. Cover and cook gently for 20 minutes or until the cabbage is just tender.

POLENTA WITH NUTS AND TOMATOES

150g/5oz corn meal (p.40)
50g/2oz walnuts
50g/2oz hazelnuts
50g/2oz brazil nuts
350g/12oz tomatoes
4 tablespoons oil
2 medium onions, thinly sliced
1 clove garlic, finely chopped
2 tablespoons chopped parsley
1 tablespoon chopped thyme
1 tablespoon chopped marjoram

Bring 900ml/1½ pints water to the boil in a saucepan. Add a pinch of salt. Turn down the heat so the water is just simmering. Pour the corn meal into the water in a thin, slow stream, stirring all the time with a wooden spoon. Stir for 20 minutes or until you have a thick "porridge" that pulls away from the sides of the pan.

Turn the polenta into a flat, ovenproof dish. Leave it for 30 minutes to cool and set. Grind or very finely chop the nuts. Scald, peel and chop the tomatoes.

Brush the top of the polenta with 1 tablespoon of the oil. Heat the grill to high. Grill under the dish of the polenta until the top browns. Keep it warm.

Heat the remaining oil in a frying pan on a low heat. Mix in the onions and garlic and soften them. Stir in the nuts, tomatoes and herbs. Cook for 5 minutes or until the tomatoes begin to soften. Pile the mixture on top of the polenta. Serve straight from the dish.

cashew nuts, curry powder, cumin and coriander. Mix in the cabbage. Pour in the stock and bring it to the boil. Cover and cook gently for 15 minutes or until the cabbage is just tender.

Take the pan from the heat. Mix in the lemon juice, yoghurt and finally the eggs.

RED CABBAGE AND ALMONDS IN CIDER

675g/1½lb red cabbage
6 black peppercorns
6 juniper berries
3 tablespoons oil
1 large onion, thinly sliced
175g/6oz whole almonds
75g/3oz raisins
175ml/6 fl oz dry cider

Finely shred the cabbage. Crush together the black peppercorns and juniper berries. Heat the oil in a saucepan over a low heat. Put in the onion and cook it for 1 minute. Raise the heat to high. Put in the cabbage and stir it on the heat for 1 minute. Add the almonds and raisins.

TAGLIATELLE WITH BEETROOT AND CHEESE SAUCE

225g/8oz wholewheat tagliatelle (p.40)
4 tablespoons olive oil
350g/12oz cooked beetroot
1 large onion, finely chopped
350g/12oz low fat soft cheese
4 tablespoons soured cream
juice of 1 lemon
2 tablespoons chopped parsley

Cook the tagliatelle in lightly salted water for 12 minutes or until it is just tender. Toss it with 2 tablespoons of the oil and keep it warm.

Finely chop the beetroot. Heat the remaining oil in a saucepan on a low heat. Put in the onion and cook it until it is just beginning to turn brown. Mix in the beetroot and heat it through. Put in the cheese and beat and stir gently for it to heat through and to mix in all the beetroot and onion. Add the soured cream and lemon juice and mix well again.

Put the tagliatelle into a serving dish. Put the beetroot and cheese sauce in a line down the centre. Scatter the parsley over the top of the sauce.

TOMATO MACARONI CHEESE

225g/8oz wholewheat macaroni
450g/1lb tomatoes
2 tablespoons chopped parsley
½ teaspoon dried mixed herbs
25g/1oz butter or vegetable margarine
2 tablespoons wholewheat flour
300ml/½ pint milk
2 tablespoons tomato purée
150g/5oz Cheddar cheese, grated

Heat the oven to 200°C/400°F/Gas 6. Cook the macaroni in lightly salted water for 15 minutes or until tender. Drain it. Scald, peel and chop the tomatoes. Mix the tomatoes, parsley and mixed herbs into the macaroni. Put them into an ovenproof dish.

Melt the butter in a saucepan on a moderate heat. Stir in the flour and milk. Bring them to the boil, stirring. Simmer for 2 minutes.

Take the pan from the heat and beat in the tomato purée and three-quarters of the cheese. Pour the sauce over the pasta and tomatoes. Scatter the remaining cheese over the top.

Put the dish into the oven for 20 minutes or until the cheese has melted and is just beginning to brown.

MUSHROOM AND MOZZARELLA RISOTTO

175g/6oz open mushrooms
225g/8oz Mozzarella cheese
3 tablespoons oil
1 large onion, thinly sliced
225g/8oz short-grain brown rice
750ml/1¼ pints Basic vegetable stock (p.6)
pinch sea salt
4 tablespoons chopped parsley
2 tablespoons grated Parmesan cheese

Thinly slice the mushrooms. Coarsely grate the Mozzarella cheese. Heat the oil in a saucepan over a low heat. Put in the onion and soften it. Put in the mushrooms and rice and stir them for 1 minute. Pour in about one-third of the stock and season with the salt. Simmer, uncovered, until nearly all the stock has been absorbed, about 15 minutes. Pour in a further third of the stock, simmer, uncovered, again for another 15 minutes or until that has nearly all been absorbed.

Add the remaining stock and simmer, uncovered, for 20 minutes or until the rice is tender and the liquid has reduced to a creamy textured glaze.

Take the pan from the heat and fork in the cheeses and the parsley. Serve as soon as possible after the cheese has been added.

Serve with either a salad or a cooked green vegetable such as broccoli or spinach.

FETA CHEESE SALAD

275g/10oz feta cheese
450g/1lb tomatoes
2 medium oranges
1 red pepper
4 tablespoons olive oil
2 tablespoons white wine vinegar
1 tablespoon tomato purée
¼ teaspoon Tabasco sauce
1 clove garlic, crushed
1 box mustard and cress

Cut the cheese into small dice. Cut the tomatoes lengthways in half and slice the halves crossways. Cut the rind and pith from the oranges. Cut each orange lengthways in half and thinly slice the halves corssways. Core and deseed the pepper. Cut it into thin, 5-cm/2-in strips. Arrange the tomatoes, oranges and peppers in a flat serving dish.

Beat together the oil, vinegar, tomato purée, Tabasco and garlic. Spoon the resulting dressing over the salad. Scatter the cheese over the top and garnish with the mustard and cress.

Serve with a rice or burghul wheat salad or with jacket potatoes.

LIGHT MEALS AND SNACKS

Vegetarian snacks are popular with everybody. Who has never enjoyed beans on toast or Welsh rarebit?

Bread can be used in other ways, too. French bread makes a delicious hot, crispy snack if it is hollowed out, given a savoury filling and baked in the oven wrapped in foil. Eat it as soon as it comes out of the oven, for if it is left standing it will lose its crispness.

Instead of sandwiches, try a bread salad. Bread soaks up dressings deliciously. Burghul wheat also makes a quick, wholegrain salad to which you can add nuts, cooked beans or diced cheese, plus salad vegetables such as celery or tomatoes.

Wholewheat pasta cooks in minutes and can be added to or topped with a light vegetable mixture that is cooked at the same time.

Scrambled eggs are a good snack-meal stand-by in most households and jacket potatoes can be topped simply with grated cheese or something more unusual such as an avocado mixture.

FRENCH BREAD FILLED WITH SPICED AUBERGINES

1 long wholewheat French loaf
350g/12oz aubergines
1 tablespoon sea salt
350g/12oz tomatoes
3 tablespoons oil
1 medium onion, finely chopped
1 clove garlic, finely chopped
1 teaspoon paprika
¼ teaspoon cinnamon
225g/8oz Mozzarella cheese

Heat the oven to 200°C/400°F/Gas 6. Cut the loaf into four equal pieces. Remove most of the crumb, leaving shells about 1cm/⅜in thick.

Cut the aubergines into 1-cm/⅜-in dice. Put them into a colander and sprinkle them with the salt. Leave them for 20 minutes to drain. Rinse them with cold water and dry them with kitchen paper. Scald, peel and chop the tomatoes.

Heat the oil in a frying pan over a low heat. Put in the onion and garlic and soften them. Put in the aubergines and sprinkle with the paprika and cinnamon. Cook for 5 minutes, stirring frequently. Mix in the tomatoes and take the pan from the heat.

Divide the filling between the bread shells. Thinly slice the Mozzarella cheese and lay the slices on top. Reshape the bread shells and wrap each one singly in a sheet of foil.

Lay the parcels on a baking sheet and put them into the oven for 20 minutes.

FRENCH BREAD FILLED WITH BEANS AND CORN

1 long wholewheat French loaf
65g/2½oz vegetable margarine or butter, softened
½ teaspoon dried mixed herbs
½ small onion
2 tablespoons wholewheat flour
200ml/7 fl oz tomato-and-vegetable juice★
one 400-g/14-oz tin red kidney beans
one 350-g/12-oz tin sweet corn
100g/4oz Cheddar cheese, grated

Heat the oven to 200°C/400°F/Gas 6. Cut the loaf into four equal pieces. Remove most of the crumb, leaving shells about 1-cm/⅜-in thick.

Beat 50g/2oz of the margarine or butter with the herbs. Grate the onion and mix well. Spread the mixture lightly over the inside of the bread shells.

Melt the remaining margarine or butter in a saucepan over a medium heat. Stir in the flour and the tomato and vegetable juice. Bring to the boil, stirring and simmer for 1–2 minutes or until you have a thick sauce. Take the pan from the heat. Drain the beans and corn and mix them into the sauce.

Divide the bean and corn mixture between the bread shells. Put a portion of the cheese on top.

Reshape the bread and wrap each shell separately in foil. Lay the parcels on a baking sheet and put them into the oven for 20 minutes.

TOMATO, BREAD AND SUNFLOWER SALAD

450g/1lb tomatoes
100g/4oz wholewheat bread
1 lemon
6 spring onions
12 black olives
4 tablespoons chopped parsley
4 tablespoons olive oil
2 tablespoons white wine vinegar
freshly ground black pepper
75g/3oz sunflower seeds★

Chop the tomatoes. Crumble the bread. Cut the rind and pith from the lemon and finely chop the flesh. Chop the spring onions. Stone and quarter the olives. Mix all these in a bowl with the parsley.

Beat together the oil, vinegar and pepper and fold the resulting dressing into the salad. Pile the salad onto a serving plate and scatter the sunflower seeds over the top.
★*Chopped walnuts* may be used instead of sunflower seeds; OR 175g/6oz feta cheese may replace the nuts.

BURGHUL, CELERY AND NUT SALAD

225g/8oz Burghul wheat (p.40)
6 celery sticks
2 dessert apples
75g/3oz hazelnuts
50g/2oz walnuts, chopped
4 tablespoons oil
2 tablespoons cider vinegar
1 clove garlic, crushed
freshly ground black pepper

Put the wheat into a bowl and cover it with warm water. Leave it to soak for 20 minutes. Drain it and squeeze it dry. Put it into a salad bowl.

Finely chop the celery. Core and chop the apples. Mix these into the wheat together with the hazelnuts and walnuts.

Beat together the oil, vinegar, garlic and pepper. Fold the resulting dressing into the salad.

BAKED POTATOES TOPPED WITH AVOCADO

4 large potatoes
225g/8oz cottage cheese
2 tablespoons soured cream
2 ripe avocados
1 clove garlic, crushed with a pinch of sea salt
4 spring onions, finely chopped
1 tablespoon Dijon mustard
8 small parsley sprigs

Heat the oven to 200°C/400°F/Gas 6. Scrub the potatoes and prick them twice on each side with a fork. Lay the potatoes on the oven rack and bake them for 1 hour 15 minutes or until they are soft in the middle and crisp on the outside.

While the potatoes are cooking, rub the cheese through a sieve and beat in the soured cream. Peel, stone and mash the avocados. Mix them into the cheese. Beat in the garlic, onions and mustard.

Cut each potato lengthways in half. Pile the avocado mixture on top and garnish with the parsley sprigs.

SPAGHETTI WITH COURGETTES AND WALNUTS

350g/12oz wholewheat spaghetti
4 tablespoons olive oil
350g/12oz courgettes, diced
1 large onion, thinly sliced
1 clove garlic, finely chopped
75g/3oz shelled walnuts

Cook the spaghetti in lightly salted water for 15 minutes or until just tender. Drain it and run cold water through it. Drain it again.

While the spaghetti is cooking, heat the oil in a saucepan over a low heat. Mix in the courgettes, onion and garlic; cover and cook for 10 minutes or until they are soft.

Grind the walnuts in a liquidiser, food processor or coffee grinder.

When the spaghetti is done, gently turn it into the courgettes and onion. Fold in the walnuts and reheat gently.

Top with grated Cheddar cheese, if wished.

GREEN PEA AND TOMATO SCRAMBLE

6 eggs
225g/8oz firm tomatoes
25g/1oz vegetable margarine or butter
1 medium onion, finely chopped
1 clove garlic, finely chopped
225g/8oz frozen peas
2 teaspoons paprika
¼ teaspoon cayenne

Lightly beat the eggs. Chop the tomatoes. (They may be scalded and peeled first, if wished.)

Melt the margarine or butter in a saucepan over a low heat. Stir in the onion, garlic and peas. Cover and cook gently for 10 minutes. Stir in the paprika and cayenne.

Pour in the eggs. Cook, stirring for about 5 minutes, or until the eggs set to a scramble. The tomatoes should be added just before the eggs set so that they heat through but stay firm.

CHEESE, POTATO AND CORN BAKE

675g/1½lb potatoes
1 large onion, thinly sliced
300ml/½ pint water
1 teaspoon yeast extract
4 tablespoons chopped parsley
150g/5oz Cheddar cheese, grated
175g/6oz cooked sweet corn
1 egg, beaten

Heat the oven to 200°C/400°C/Gas 6. Peel the potatoes and cut them into 1.5-cm/½-in dice. Put them into a saucepan with the onion, water and yeast extract. Bring them to the boil. Cover and cook them gently for 15 minutes or until they are soft and all the water has been absorbed.

Mash the potatoes with the onion. Mix in the parsley, about three-quarters of the cheese, the sweet corn and the egg.

Put the mixture into an ovenproof dish and scatter the remaining cheese over the top. Bake for 20 minutes or until the cheese on top has melted and is beginning to brown.

BAKED JULIENNE OF CARROTS AND ONIONS

675g/1½lbs carrots
2 small onions
4 tablespoons oil
2 tablespoons tomato purée
1 teaspoon paprika
1 clove garlic, finely chopped
2 tablespoons thyme, chopped
sea salt

Heat the oven to 180°C/350°F/Gas 4. Cut the carrots and onions into matchstick-sized pieces. In a bowl, mix together the oil, tomato purée and paprika. Mix in the carrots, onions, garlic and thyme. Season lightly.

Divide the mixture between four 30-cm/12-in square pieces of foil. Seal the edges of the foil together along the top and then fold the ends upwards.

Lay the parcels on a baking sheet and put them into the oven for 45 minutes.

ONIONS WITH ORANGE STUFFING

4 175g/6oz onions
25g/1oz butter
1 tablespoon chopped parsley
1 tablespoon chopped thyme
100g/4oz wholewheat bread crumbs
grated rind and juice of 1 medium orange
2 teaspoons Dijon mustard
200ml/7fl oz Basic vegetable stock (p.6)

Heat the oven to 180°C/350°F/Gas 4. Peel the onions. Cut a small slice from the top of each one about 1cm/½in thick. Using a teaspoon and a small, sharp knife, remove the centres of the onions leaving shells about 5mm/¼in thick. Finely chop half the scooped out onion. Discard the rest.

Melt the butter in a frying pan over a low heat. Put in the chopped onion and cook it until it is soft but not coloured. Take the pan from the heat and mix in the herbs, breadcrumbs, orange rind and juice and mustard. Pack the mixture into the onions. Stand the onions in a casserole.

Bring the stock to the boil and pour it round the onions. Cover the casserole and put it into the oven for 1 hour.

BRUSSELS SPROUTS WITH BLACK OLIVES

450g/1lb Brussels sprouts
12 black olives
3 tablespoons olive oil
1 clove garlic, finely chopped
150ml/¼ pint dry red wine

Trim the Brussels sprouts and cut them into 5-mm/
¼-in thick slices. Stone and quarter the olives.

Heat the oil in a large frying pan over a medium
heat. Put in the Brussels sprouts and garlic and stir
them for 2 minutes. Add the olives. Pour in the wine
and bring it to the boil. Cover and cook over a low
heat for 10 minutes.

JACKET POTATOES WITH SOURED CREAM AND DILL

4 large baking potatoes
4 tablespoons soured cream
2 teaspoons dill seeds

Heat the oven to 200°C/400°F/Gas 6. Scrub the
potatoes and prick each one on both sides with a fork.
Lay the potatoes on the oven rack and bake them for 1
hour 15 minutes or until the middles are soft and the
outsides crisp.

Cut each potato in half lengthways and scoop the
flesh into a bowl. Mash it. Add the soured cream and
dill seeds and mix well. Pile the mixture back into the
potato shells.

Lay the shells on an ovenproof plate or dish.
Return them to the oven for 20 minutes or until the
tops are golden brown.

SALADS, DRESSINGS & VEGETABLES

You don't have to be a vegetarian to enjoy vegetables, but vegetarians often make most use of them. Rather than simply a dull accompaniment, vegetables should be treated with just as much care as the main dish. They too can be cooked with herbs, spices, olives or nuts. They can be baked, simmered, braised, stir-fried, or eaten raw in a crunchy salad.

If possible, always use fresh vegetables, which contain more goodness than the frozen or tinned varieties. Store them for as short a time as possible and prepare them just before they are to be cooked. Serve several different types of vegetable at every meal. This ensures that you get a wide range of nutrients and makes your meal more enjoyable.

Whichever way you cook, you will inevitably destroy some vitamins. Hence try to eat a salad every day, either with the main meal of with a snack meal at lunch or supper time. Salads don't have to consist of limp lettuce leaves, cucumber rings and half a tomato. Nearly every vegetable can be served raw. Combine several vegetables; add fried fruits, fresh fruits and nuts, and mix everything with a tasty dressing. Then you will have a salad to please everybody.

BASIC FRENCH DRESSING

4 tablespoons oil
2 tablespoons wine vinegar
freshly ground black pepper
pinch of salt (optional)

Either beat the ingredients together well or put them into a bottle and shake them. Larger amounts may be made up and stored in a bottle in the refrigerator. Always shake the bottle before use.

Vinegars to Use:
white wine vinegar
red wine vinegar
sherry vinegar
cider vinegar
flavoured vinegars, e.g.
  tarragon, lemon,
  chilli or other herb
  vinegars
  (Malt vinegar should
  only be used where a
  strong flavour is
  required.)

Oils to Use:
olive
sunflower
safflower
groundnut
corn
soya
sesame
walnut

Alternatives:
lemon juice
orange juice, preferably
  freshly squeezed
half vinegar may be
  replaced by wine for a
  milder flavour

Flavourings for Dressing:
1 clove garlic, crushed (an essential ingredient in
  most salads)
up to 2 tablespoons chopped fresh herbs
up to 2 teaspoons dried herbs
1 teaspoon mustard powder
1 teaspoon Dijon or other spiced mustard
1 tablespoon tomato purée
1 tablespoon soy sauce
1 tablespoon Worcestershire sauce
1 teaspoon paprika
1 teaspoon paprika plus pinch of cayenne OR ¼
  teaspoon Tabasco sauce
½ teaspoon cinnamon
½ teaspoon curry powder
¼ teaspoon curry paste
½ teaspoon each ground cumin and coriander
1 teaspoon dill seeds
When adding ground spices, whole seeds, or dried
  herbs, it is best to let the dressing stand for 30
  minutes before using.

MAYONNAISE

1 egg yolk
½ teaspoon mustard powder
freshly ground pepper (white is often preferred
  for the colour)
125ml/4 fl oz not too highly flavoured oil such
  as sunflower
1 tablespoon white wine vinegar

Beat the egg yolk in a bowl. Beat in the mustard powder and pepper. Drop by drop, beat in 1 tablespoon of the oil, then 1 teaspoon of the vinegar and then, very slowly, the remaining oil. Taste the mayonnaise and add the remaining vinegar a little at a time until the required flavour is reached. Some like it more sharp than others.

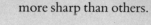

YOGHURT MAYONNAISE

Make as above using only the first teaspoon of vinegar, 4 tablespoons oil and 4 tablespoons natural yoghurt which should be beaten in after the oil.

Yoghurt's sharp flavour makes the extra vinegar unnecessary.

Flavourings for Mayonnaise:

replace the mustard powder with 1 teaspoon spiced
  coarse-grain mustard or Dijon mustard, OR ½
  teaspoon curry paste
1 clove garlic, crushed, added to egg yolks before oil
½ small onion, grated, added to egg yolks before oil
1 tablespoon tomato purée, added after the first
  vinegar
4–6 tablespoons chopped parsley added after making
2 chopped dill pickles or pickled gherkins, added after
  making

Yoghurt Dressings

Yoghurt may be used alone as a dressing or it may be enriched with oil. To 4 tablespoons natural yoghurt, add 2 tablespoons oil and beat well.

Any of the following may be added to 6 tablespoons natural yoghurt or the yoghurt-oil mixture:

1 teaspoon honey plus 1 tablespoon lemon juice OR
  wine vinegar
1 clove garlic, crushed
1 tablespoon tomato purée
1 teaspoon spiced coarse-grain mustard or Dijon
  mustard
1 tablespoon Tahini (sesame paste, see page 13)
1 teaspoon paprika
1 teaspoon paprika plus pinch of cayenne OR ¼
  teaspoon Tabasco sauce
½ teaspoon cinnamon
½ teaspoon each ground cumin and coriander
½ teaspoon turmeric
4 tablespoons chopped parsley
up to 2 tablespoons other chopped herbs (chervil,
  dill, fennel, basil)
1 tablespoon poppy seeds

CABBAGE, GRAPE AND RAISIN SALAD

½ medium-sized white cabbage
100g/4oz white grapes
50g/2oz raisins
4 tablespoons olive or sunflower oil
2 tablespoons white wine vinegar
1 teaspoon coarse-grain white wine mustard
1 clove garlic, crushed
freshly ground black pepper

Finely shred the cabbage and put it into a salad bowl. Halve and seed the grapes and mix them into the cabbage with the raisins.

Beat the remaining ingredients together to make the dressing and fold into the salad.

CELERY, RADISH AND APPLE SALAD

1 head celery
175g/6oz radishes
1 dessert apple
6 tablespoons natural yoghurt
2 teaspoons cider vinegar
1 teaspoon honey
1 clove garlic, crushed

Finely chop the celery. Thinly slice the radishes. Core and chop the apple. Put them all into a bowl.

Beat together the remaining ingredients and fold the resulting dressing into the salad.

BEAN SPROUT AND MUSHROOM SALAD

250g/8oz bean sprouts
100g/4oz button mushrooms
4 tablespoons sesame oil (or sunflower oil if
    none is available)
juice of ½ lemon
1 tablespoon soy sauce
1 teaspoon honey
½ teaspoon ginger
1 tablespoon sesame seeds

Put the beansprouts into a salad bowl. Thinly slice
the mushrooms and mix them with the bean sprouts.

Beat together the oil, lemon juice, soy sauce,
honey and ginger. Mix them into the beans sprouts
and mushrooms.

Put the sesame seeds into a heavy frying pan,
without fat or oil. Set them on a moderate heat and
stir them around until they brown and start to jump
about. Tip them immediately onto a cool plate.
When they are cold, scatter them over the salad.

TOMATO AND RED PEPPER SALAD

450g/1lb tomatoes
2 medium-sized red peppers
50g/2oz currants
2 black olives
4 tablespoons oil
2 tablespoons white wine vinegar
¼ teaspoon Tabasco sauce
1 clove garlic, crushed

Cut the tomatoes into thin rounds. Core, deseed and
finely chop the pepper. Put the peppers in a pile in the
centre of a serving plate. Arrange the tomato rings
round the edge. Scatter the currants over the
tomatoes only. Halve and stone the olives and put
them on top of the peppers as a garnish.

Beat together the oil, vinegar, Tabasco and garlic.
Sprinkle the resulting dressing over the salad.

CUCUMBER AND BLUE CHEESE SALAD

1 large cucumber
50g/2oz soft blue cheese
4 tablespoons natural yoghurt
1 clove garlic, crushed
pinch of cayenne
½ teaspoon paprika

Cut half the cucumber into thin slices. Chop the rest into 5-mm/¼-in cubes. Cream the cheese in a bowl and gradually work in the yoghurt. Mix in the garlic and cayenne.

Arrange the cucumber slices in overlapping circles around the edge of a serving plate. Mix the diced cucumber into the cheese dressing and then spoon it into the centre of the cucumber rings.

Scatter the paprika over the top of the diced cucumber.

CABBAGE WITH APPLE AND GREEN PEPPERS

1 small green cabbage
1 medium cooking apple
1 large OR 2 small green peppers
3 tablespoons oil
1 medium onion, thinly sliced
1 clove garlic, finely chopped
125ml/4 fl oz Basic vegetable stock (p. 6)

Shred the cabbage. Peel, core and slice the apple. Core and seed the peppers and cut them into 2.5-cm/1-in strips.

Heat the oil in a saucepan over a high heat. Mix in the cabbage, apple, peppers, onion and garlic. Stir them for 1 minute. Pour in the stock and bring it to the boil.

Cover and cook on a low heat for 15 minutes or until the cabbage is just tender.

TOMATOES BAKED WITH MIXED NUTS

450g/1lb tomatoes
1 tablespoon oil
1 tablespoon white wine vinegar
1 clove garlic, crushed
4 tablespoons chopped parsley
4 tablespoons mixed nuts, chopped

Heat the oven to 200°C/400°F/Gas 6. Scald and peel the tomatoes and cut them crossways into 5-mm/¼-in slices. Put them into a flat ovenproof dish.

Beat together the oil, vinegar and garlic. Scatter the mixture over the tomatoes. Mix together the parsley and nuts and sprinkle them over the top.

Bake the tomatoes for 15 minutes or until the nuts just begin to brown.

SPICED AUBERGINE AND COURGETTE KEBABS

350g/12oz aubergines
350g/12oz courgettes
6 tablespoons olive oil
juice of ½ lemon
1 clove garlic, crushed
1 teaspoon ground cumin
1 teaspoon ground coriander

Cut the aubergines and courgettes into 2.5-cm/1-in dice. In a large bowl, beat the remaining ingredients together. Fold in the vegetables and leave them for 30 minutes.

Heat the grill to high. Thread alternate pieces of the vegetables onto kebab skewers. Grill them, turning them twice, so they are browned on all sides, for about 10 minutes altogether.

GRAIN ACCOMPANIMENTS

Grains and vegetable protein foods are the perfect partners in every way. If you are serving a meal based on pulses or nuts, a grain accompaniment is essential if your body is to absorb the right type of protein. You will also find that it is the right combination for enjoyment.

Whole grains are exactly what the name implies: they are the unpolished seeds of various plants, complete with their outer coating of bran and their inner core of vitamins and minerals.

Brown rice is the grain most associated with vegetarian cooking. Long-grain or short-grain varieties are available from most supermarkets and health food shops. **Wholewheat pasta** is another readily available grain product. Look for spaghetti, macaroni, rings, spirals, shells and tagliatelle.

Millet is not only for the birds. The tiny, round, yellow seeds cook to give a fluffy grain dish that is light both in texture and flavour.

Buckwheat is a tiny, brown, heart-shaped seed with a distinctly nutty flavour. The dish made from it is often referred to as **kasha.**

Pot barley is simply whole barley grains, unlike pearl barley which has been stripped of the outer bran.

Burghul wheat is the product of whole wheat grains that have been soaked in water and then heated until they break into tiny yellow particles. It is mainly used for salads. It does not have to be cooked but should be soaked in warm water for 20 minutes, drained and squeezed dry before being mixed with other ingredients into a dressing.

Polenta is a type of porridge made from **corn meal.** This is a coarse yellow flour made by the grinding of sweet corn kernels.

PLAIN BROWN RICE

225g/8oz long-grain brown rice
600ml/1 pint water
pinch of sea salt

Put the rice into a saucepan with the water and salt. Bring it slowly to the boil. Cover and cook gently for 40–45 minutes or until the rice is soft and all the water has been absorbed.

BROWN RICE WITH PARSLEY AND LEMON

225g/8oz long-grain brown rice
3 tablespoons olive oil
1 medium onion, thinly sliced
1 clove garlic, finely chopped
4 tablespoons chopped parsley
juice of ½ lemon

Plainly cook the rice as above. Run cold water through it and drain it well. Heat the oil in a frying pan on a low heat. Put in the onion and garlic and cook them until the onion is just beginning to brown. Raise the heat to moderate. Fork in the rice and parsley. When they are heated through, pour in the lemon juice and mix well.

SPICED APPLE RICE

1 large cooking apple
3 tablespoons oil
1 medium onion, thinly sliced
225g/8oz long-grain brown rice
1 teaspoon ground cumin
600ml/1 pint Basic vegetable stock
   (p.6)

Peel, core and slice the apple. Heat the oil in a saucepan on a slow heat. Put in the apple and onion and cook them until the onion is beginning to soften. Stir in rice and cumin. Cook them for 1 minute.

Pour in the stock and bring it to the boil. Cover and cook gently for 45 minutes or until the rice is tender and all the water has been absorbed. Take the pan from the heat and leave the rice to stand, still covered, for 5 minutes.

RICE AND RED PEPPER SALAD

225g/8oz long-grain brown rice
1 large red pepper
One 175-g/6-oz tin sweet corn
4 tomatoes
1 orange
4 tablespoons oil
2 tablespoons white wine vinegar
1 tablespoon tomato purée
1 clove garlic, crushed
¼ teaspoon Tabasco sauce

Plainly cook the rice as above. Run cold water through it and drain it well. Leave it to cool.

Core, deseed and finely chop the pepper. Drain the sweet corn. Chop the tomatoes. Cut the rind and pith from the orange. Halve it lengthways and cut each half into three lengthways pieces. Thinly slice them. Mix the pepper, corn, tomatoes and orange into the rice.

Beat together the oil, vinegar, tomato purée, garlic and Tabasco. Fold the resulting dressing into the salad.

BARLEY BAKE WITH CARROTS

350g/12oz carrots
1 large onion
2 tablespoons oil
225g/8oz pot barley
600ml/1 pint Basic vegetable stock (p. 6)
1 tablespoon chopped thyme OR 1 teaspoon dried
1 tablespoon chopped marjoram OR 1 teaspoon dried
pinch of sea salt
freshly ground black pepper
4 tablespoons chopped parsley

Heat the oven to 180°C/350°F/Gas 4. Finely chop the carrots and onion.

Heat the oil in a flameproof casserole over a low heat. Stir in the carrots and onion. Cover and cook them gently for 5 minutes. Stir in the barley. Pour in the stock and bring it to the boil. Add the thyme, marjoram and seasonings.

Cover the casserole and put it into the oven for 45 minutes or until the barley is tender and all the stock has been absorbed.

Mix in the parsley just before serving.

BURGHUL AND GREEN OLIVE SALAD

225g/8oz burghul wheat (p. 40)
12 green olives
6 spring onions
4 tablespoons chopped parsley
4 tablespoons olive oil
juice of ½ lemon
freshly ground black pepper
tomato wedges (optional)

Soak the wheat in warm water for 20 minutes. Drain it and squeeze it dry. Put it into a bowl. Stone and quarter eight of the olives. Cut the spring onions into 1-cm/½-in pieces. Add the olives, onions and parsley to the wheat.

Beat together the oil, lemon juice and pepper. Fold the resulting dressing into the salad.

Halve and stone the remaining olives and use them as a garnish; also garnish with tomato wedges, if desired.

CURRIED MILLET WITH MUSHROOMS

100g/4oz mushrooms
3 tablespoons oil
1 medium onion, thinly sliced
1 clove garlic, finely chopped
225g/8oz millet
2 teaspoons curry powder
600ml/1 pint Basic vegetable stock (p.6)

Thinly slice the mushrooms. Heat the oil in a saucepan on a low heat. Put in the onion and garlic and soften them. Stir in the millet, mushrooms and curry powder. Cook them, stirring frequently, for 1 minute.

Pour in the stock and bring it to the boil. Cover and cook gently for 20 minutes or until the millet is soft and fluffy and all the stock has been absorbed.

KASHA WITH CELERY AND YOGHURT

225g/8oz buckwheat groats (p.40)
1 egg, beaten
600ml/1 pint Basic vegetable stock (p.6)
4 celery sticks, finely chopped
1 medium onion, thinly sliced
150ml/¼ pint natural yoghurt
4 tablespoons chopped parsley

Put the buckwheat into a frying pan and set it over a moderate heat. Stir until it begins to brown. Pour in the egg and quickly stir so that it sets round the grains. Pour in the stock and bring it to the boil. Put in the celery and onion. Cover and cook gently for 15 minutes or until the buckwheat is soft and fluffy.

Remove from heat. Stir in the yoghurt and keep stirring until it is no longer visible. Mix in the parsley.

PLAIN POLENTA

900ml/1½ pints water
¼ teaspoon salt
150g/5oz corn meal

Put the water into a saucepan and bring it to the boil. Put in the salt and turn down the heat so that the water is barely simmering. Pour the corn meal into the water in a thin, slow stream, stirring all the time with a wooden spoon. Stir for about 20 minutes or until you have a thick "porridge" which will pull away from the sides of the pan.

The polenta can be served as it is or can be flavoured with herbs, cheese or vegetables.

POLENTA WITH ONIONS AND TOMATOES

Basic recipe for polenta as above
2 medium onions
225g/8oz tomatoes
3 tablespoons oil
1 clove garlic, chopped
1 tablespoon chopped thyme, OR ½ teaspoon dried

Thinly slice the onions. Scald and peel the tomatoes and cut them into wedges. Heat the oil in a frying pan over a low heat. Put in the onions and garlic and soften them. Add the tomatoes and thyme and cook for 2 minutes so that the tomatoes are heated through but still firm.

When the polenta is cooked, mix in the onions and tomatoes.

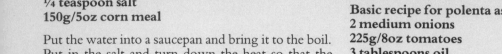

SPAGHETTI WITH MIXED VEGETABLE SAUCE

225g/8oz wholewheat spaghetti
350g/12oz tomatoes
3 celery sticks
100g/4oz carrots
1 medium onion
3 tablespoons oil
1 clove garlic, finely chopped
1 teaspoon dried mixed herbs

Cook the spaghetti in lightly salted boiling water for 12 minutes or until just tender. Drain it; run warm water through it and keep it warm.

Scald, peel and finely chop the tomatoes. Finely chop the celery. Finely grate the carrot. Finely chop the onion.

Heat the oil in a saucepan over a low heat. Put in the celery, carrot, onion and garlic. Cover and cook gently for 10 minutes. Put in the tomatoes and herbs. Cover and cook for a further 10 minutes.

The spaghetti may be either gently folded into the sauce, or put onto a serving plate and the sauce spooned over the top.

This sauce can also be used for tagliatelle and other types of wholewheat pasta.

PASTA WITH PEAS AND CURD CHEESE

225g/8oz wholewheat pasta shells or spirals
15g/½oz butter
1 medium onion, thinly sliced
125ml/4 fl oz Basic vegetable stock (p.6)
75g/3oz curd cheese
100g/4oz cooked peas, fresh or frozen
4 tablespoons chopped parsley

Cook the pasta in lightly salted water for 12 minutes or until it is just tender. Drain it; run warm water through it and drain it again.

Melt the butter in a saucepan over a low heat. Put in the onion and cook it until it is golden. Pour in the stock and bring it to the boil. Take the pan from the heat. Add the cheese in small pieces and beat well to make a smooth, thick sauce.

Gently fold in the pasta, peas and parsley. Set the pan back over a low heat. Stir carefully so the peas and pasta heat through but do not boil.

BAKING

The basic vegetarian baking techniques are the same as those used in any other form of wholefood baking. Use wholewheat (also called wholemeal) flour for everything. It will provide you with fibre, some B vitamins, vitamin E and important minerals such as calcium and iron, all in the right proportions; and, contrary to what you may believe, it is easy to use and will give excellent results. Pastry will be crisp, bread light and tasty and easy to cut. Cakes will not be quite as light and airy as those made with white flour and caster sugar; however, the delicious flavour compensates for that, standing by itself without the need for sugary toppings.

SCONE-BASED MUSHROOM PIZZA

Base:
225g/8oz wholewheat flour
1 teaspoon fine sea salt
1 teaspoon bicarbonate of soda
3 tablespoons olive oil
150ml/¼ pint natural yoghurt

Heat the oven to 200°C/400°/Gas 6. Put the flour into a bowl with the salt and bicarbonate of soda. Make a well in the centre and put in the oil and yoghurt. Mix everything to a dough. Turn the dough onto a floured work surface and knead it lightly until it is smooth.

Roll out the dough to a 27-cm/11-in round and put it into a 25-cm/10-in pizza tin or pizza plate. Fold over the edges. Prick the base all over with a fork.

Top:
225g/8oz open mushrooms
1 red pepper
1 medium onion
12 black olives
4 tablespoons oil
1 clove garlic, finely chopped
1 tablespoon chopped thyme
1 tablespoon chopped marjoram
150ml/¼ pint tomato juice
225g/8oz Edam cheese
2 tomatoes

Thinly slice the mushrooms. Core and deseed the pepper and cut it into 2.5-cm/1-in strips. Thinly slice the onion. Halve and stone the olives. Cut eight into quarters. Reserve the other halves.

Heat the oil in a frying pan on a low heat. Put in the mushrooms, pepper, onions, garlic and herbs. Cover and cook gently for 10 minutes. Raise the heat. Pour

in the tomato juice and bring it to the boil. Add the quartered olives. Boil rapidly, stirring, for about 4 minutes, or until most of the tomato juice has evaporated.

Put the mushroom mixture onto the scone base. Thinly slice the cheese and lay it over the top. Cut each tomato into four slices. Garnish the pizza with these and with the olive halves.

Bake the pizza for 25 minutes or until the edges are just beginning to colour and the cheese has melted. Serve hot.

CHEESY SCONE WHIRLS

225g/8oz wholewheat flour
½ teaspoon fine sea salt
½ teaspoon bicarbonate of soda
1 teaspoon dried mixed herbs
3 tablespoons corn oil
150ml/¼ pint natural yoghurt, buttermilk, OR sour milk
2 tablespoons tomato purée
175g/6oz Cheddar cheese, finely grated

Heat the oven to 200°C/400°C/Gas 6. Put the flour into a mixing bowl. Toss in the salt, soda and herbs. Make a well in the centre. Pour in the oil and yoghurt (or buttermilk or sour milk). Mix everything to a dough. Turn it onto a floured work-top and knead it lightly to make it smooth.

Roll the dough out to an oblong about 25×30cm/ 10×12in. Spread it with the tomato purée and scatter half the cheese over the top. Roll up the dough from one narrow end. Trim each end flat if necessary and then cut the roll into 2.5-cm/1-in thick slices.

Lay the rounds on a floured baking sheet. Bake them for 10 minutes. Scatter the remaining cheese over the top and return the rounds to the oven for a further 5 minutes.

Lift the rounds onto a wire rack. They may be either eaten warm or left to cool.

WHOLEWHEAT BREAD

25g/1oz fresh OR 15g/½oz dried yeast
300ml/½ pint warm water
1 teaspoon honey (for dried yeast only)
2 teaspoons sea salt
450g/1lb wholewheat flour
1 egg, beaten (optional)

If you are using fresh yeast, crumble it into a bowl and pour in half the water. If you are using dried, dissolve the honey in half the water and sprinkle in the yeast. Leave the yeast in a warm place to froth, about 10 minutes for fresh yeast, 20 minutes for dried.

Dissolve the salt in the remaining water. Put the flour into a bowl and make a well in the centre. Pour in the yeast mixture and mix in a little flour from the sides of the well. Pour in the salt water and mix everything together.

Turn the dough onto a floured work surface and knead it until it is smooth and no longer feels sticky. Return it to the bowl. Cover it with a clean tea cloth and leave it in a warm place for 1 hour or until it has doubled in size.

Heat the oven to 200°C/400°F/Gas 6. Oil a 900-g/2-lb loaf tin. Turn the dough onto the work surface again and knead it lightly. Shape it into a loaf and put it into the prepared tin. If wished, brush the top with beaten egg. Cover the dough with the tea cloth again and leave it for about 20 minutes, or until it has risen to about 1.5cm/½in above the top of the tin.

Bake the loaf for 50 minutes. Turn it onto a wire rack and cool it completely before slicing.

Decorations: After brushing with beaten egg the loaf may be scattered with cracked wheat, sesame seeds or poppy seeds.

Loaf shapes: Instead of baking it in a tin, try forming the loaf into varying shapes and baking it on a floured baking sheet.

Cobber: Form the dough into a round.

Bloomer: Form the dough into an oval and slash the top diagonally three times after brushing with the egg.

Cottage Loaf: Divide the dough into one-third and two-thirds pieces. Set the smaller one on top of the larger one. Push the rounded handle of a wooden spoon down through the two and flatten them slightly to keep them steady.

Plait: Divide the dough into three equal portions. Roll each one into a long stick. Join them all at one end, plait them twice or three times and join them at the other end. If wished, the dough can be divided into one-third and two-thirds and a small plait placed on top of a larger one.

Small Rolls: Form the dough into 12 small rounds. Lay them on a floured baking sheet and flatten them slightly. Bake them for 20 minutes.

NUT-FILLED BRIOCHES

25g/1oz fresh OR 15g/½oz dried yeast
1 teaspoon honey (for dried yeast only)
4 tablespoons warm water
350g/12oz flour
1 teaspoon fine sea salt
3 eggs, beaten
6 tablespoons oil
beaten egg for glaze

Filling:
25g/1oz walnuts
25g/1oz hazelnuts
50g/2oz brazil nuts
2 celery sticks
1 medium onion
2 tablespoons oil
1 clove garlic, finely chopped
4 tablespoons chopped parsley
1 tablespoon chopped thyme
4 tablespoons dry red wine OR Basic vegetable
    stock (p.6)

If you are using fresh yeast, crumble it into a bowl
and pour in the warm water. If you are using dried,
dissolve the honey in the water and sprinkle in the
yeast. Leave the yeast in a warm place to froth.

Put the flour into a bowl and toss in the salt. Make
a well in the centre. Pour in the yeast mixture and stir
a little of the flour into it. Stir in the beaten eggs and
oil. Mix everything to a dough. Turn it onto a
floured work surface and knead it until it is smooth.
Return it to the bowl and make a cross-cut in the top.
Cover the dough with a clean tea cloth and leave it in
a warm place for 1 hour or until it has doubled in size.

To make the filling, coarsely grind the nuts using a
blender, food processor or coffee grinder. Finely
chop the celery and onion. Heat the oil in a frying pan
on a low heat. Put in the celery, onion and garlic and
soften them. Mix in the nuts, parsley and thyme.
Take the pan from the heat and mix in the wine. Let
the mixture cool.

Heat the oven to 200°C/400°F/Gas 6. Knead the
dough again and divide it into eight portions. Roll
each piece into a round about 5mm/¼in thick. Put a
portion of the filling in the centre. Bring the edges of
the dough to the centre and seal them by pinching
them together. Turn the dough over and form it into
a round bun with the sealed edges underneath.

Either lay the buns on a floured baking sheet or put
them into small, oiled brioche moulds. Leave them in
a warm place for 15 minutes or until they have almost
doubled in size.

Bake the brioches for 20 minutes or until they are
golden. Lift them onto a wire rack. Serve them warm
if possible.

SHORTCRUST PASTRY

225g/8oz wholewheat flour
pinch of fine sea salt
125g/4oz vegetable margarine or butter, softened
5 tablespoons cold water

Put the flour and salt into a bowl. Put in the margarine or butter and water. Using a fork, gradually mix them into the flour, using a stirring motion. Press the mixture together with your fingers.

Form the dough into a ball. Coat it lightly with extra wholewheat flour. Leave it in a cool place for 30 minutes before rolling.

Savoury Additions:
1–2 teaspoons dried mixed herbs
1 teaspoon any dried herb but bay
2–3 tablespoons chopped parsley
1 teaspoon mustard powder
1 teaspoon paprika
1 teaspoon paprika plus ¼ teaspoon cayenne
½ teaspoon ground cumin and coriander

Sweet Additions:
Freshly grated nutmeg (about ¼ nut)
1 teaspoon ground mixed spice
1 teaspoon cinnamon
½ teaspoon ground cloves

CARROT AND WALNUT QUICHE

Use this recipe for Shortcrust pastry plus 1 teaspoon dried mixed herbs.

350g/12oz carrots
50g/2oz walnuts
4 tablespoons oil
1 large onion, finely chopped
1 clove garlic, finely chopped
¼ nutmeg, freshly grated
4 tablespoons chopped parsley
4 eggs
150ml/¼ pint milk

Heat the oven to 200°C/400°F/Gas 6. Roll out the pastry and use it to line a 25-cm/10-in diameter tart tin.

Finely grate the carrots. Finely chop or coarsely grind the walnuts. Heat the oil in a saucepan over a low heat. Put in the carrots, onion and garlic, and grate in the nutmeg. Cover and cook over a low heat for 10 minutes. Take the pan from the heat and mix in the walnuts and parsley. Cool slightly.

Arrange the carrot mixture in an even layer in the pastry shell. Beat together the eggs and milk and pour them over the carrots.

Bake the quiche for 30 minutes or until the filling is set and lightly browned.

MIXED PEPPER TART

Cheese Pastry:
225g/8oz wholewheat flour
pinch of fine sea salt
1 teaspoon mustard powder
50g/2oz butter, softened or vegetable margarine
125g/4oz curd cheese OR *fromage blanc*
1 egg yolk
1 tablespoon cold water

Filling:
2 large green peppers
2 large red peppers
1 large onion
3 tablespoons oil
1 clove garlic, finely chopped
225g/8oz curd cheese OR *fromage blanc*
4 eggs, beaten
2 tablespoons chopped parsley
1 tablespoon chopped thyme

Put the flour and salt into a bowl. Rub in the butter and cheese. Make a well in the centre and put in the egg yolk and water. Bring the mixture together to form a dough. Set the dough aside in a cool place for 30 minutes before using.

Heat the oven to 200°C/400°F/Gas 6. Core and deseed the peppers and cut them into strips. Thinly slice the onion. Heat the oil in a frying pan on a low heat. Put in the peppers, onion and garlic and cook them until the onion is beginning to turn golden. Take them from the heat and cool them slightly.

Put the cheese into a bowl. Add the eggs a little at a time, beating well after each addition. Beat in the parsley and thyme.

Roll out the pastry and line a 25-cm/10-in tart tin. Put in the peppers and onion and spread them out evenly. Pour in the cheese mixture. Bake the tart for 30 minutes or until the filling is set and golden. Serve hot or cold.

DATE AND PEANUT TEA BREAD

225g/8oz stoned dates
225g/8oz wholewheat flour
1 teaspoon bicarbonate of soda
½ teaspoon salt
75g/3oz crunchy peanut butter
75g/3oz honey
1 egg, beaten
150ml/¼ pint milk

Heat the oven to 170°C/325°F/Gas 3. Finely chop the dates. Mix together the flour, bicarbonate of soda and salt.

Put the peanut butter into a bowl and gradually beat in first the honey and then the egg. Mix in the flour and beat in the milk. Add the dates and mix well.

Put the mixture into a well–greased 450–g/1–lb loaf tin and bake it for 1 hour or until a skewer stuck in the centre comes out clean. Turn the loaf onto a wire rack to cool.

Serve the loaf plainly, cut into thin slices.

APRICOT ALMOND AND CHERRY CAKES

125g/4oz dried whole apricots
225ml/8 fl oz apple juice
50g/2oz glacé cherries plus 4 extra for garnish
125g/4oz wholewheat flour
25g/1oz almonds, ground
1 teaspoon bicarbonate of soda
4 tablespoons corn oil
4 tablespoons natural yoghurt

Put the apricots into a saucepan with the apple juice. Bring them to the boil. Take them from the heat and leave them to soak for 4 hours. Drain the apricots and then liquidise them with 4 tablespoons of the juice. Oil 16 bun tins. Heat the oven to 180°C/350°F/Gas 4.

Finely chop the 50g/2oz cherries. Put the flour, almonds and bicarbonate of soda into a bowl. Mix in the chopped cherries. Make a well in the centre and put in the liquidised apricots, corn oil and yoghurt. Beat everything together to make a mixture with a dripping consistency.

Divide the mixture between the bun tins. Garnish each cake with a cherry quarter. Bake the cakes for 15 minutes or until firm and just beginning to colour.

ALL-IN-ONE WHOLEWHEAT CAROB CAKE

175g/6oz wholewheat flour
1 teaspoon baking powder
25g/1oz carob powder, sieved
175g/6oz vegetable margarine plus extra for greasing
175g/6oz Barbados sugar
3 eggs beaten

Filling:
225/8oz curd cheese
2 tablespoons clear honey
2 tablespoons carob powder, sieved

Decoration
2 tablespoons flaked almonds

Heat the oven to 180°C/350°F/Gas 4. Grease two 18-cm/7-in sponge tins. Put the flour, baking powder and carob powder into a bowl. Mix well. Make a well in the centre. Put in the remaining ingredients and beat well with a wooden spoon until the mixture is smooth.

Divide the mixture between the two prepared sponge tins and bake the cakes for 20 minutes or until firm. Cool them in tins for 5 minutes and turn them onto wire racks to cool.

For the filling, beat the honey and carob powder into the curd cheese. Sandwich the cakes together with one-third of the mixture and spread the rest over the top and sides. Scatter the almonds over the top.

PLAIN WHOLEWHEAT SPONGE CAKE

175g/6oz wholewheat flour
1 teaspoon bicarbonate of soda
175g/6oz vegetable margarine
175g/6oz Barbados sugar (light or dark)
3 eggs, beaten

Heat the oven to 180°C/350°F/Gas 4. Toss the flour with the bicarbonate of soda. Beat the margarine and sugar together in a bowl. Gradually beat in the eggs, alternating them with the flour.

Divide the mixture between two greased 18-cm/7-in diameter sponge tins. Bake the cakes for 20 minutes or until they are firm and springy and have shrunk slightly from the sides of the tins.

Variations:
The sugar may be replaced by 150g/5oz honey. The margarine may be replaced by 6 tablespoons each corn oil and natural orange juice, in which case, put the flour and sugar into the bowl first. Then add all the liquid ingredients and beat to make a thick batter. Allow 30 minutes cooking time. 1 teaspoon ground mixed spice or the grated rind of 1 lemon or orange may be added to the flour.

Fillings for sponge cake:
A thick layer of sugar-free jam
125g/4oz curd cheese or low fat soft cheese beaten with 2 tablespoons honey or sugar-free jam (allow double quantity if it is to be spread on the top as well)
50g/2oz dried whole apricots, simmered in fruit juice until soft and puréed
Any soft fruits in season, placed on a bed of whipped cream or curd cheese beaten with honey.

DESSERTS

No one need be deprived of sweets simply because the rest of their diet is vegetarian; however, desserts are best regarded as treats to be served occasionally—perhaps only at weekends—rather than as a necessity at every meal time. On most other days, follow meals with lighter things such as fresh fruits in season or natural yoghurt.

The one big difference between vegetarian desserts and others is that gelatin is not used. If you still include meat meals between your vegetarian ones then this will not worry you, but if you wish to be completely vegetarian you will have to use a substitute.

In the health food shop you will find a substance called **agar-agar.** It is a Japanese product, made by drying a certain type of seaweed. The result is a translucent, white, crystal-like or powered substance which will dissolve in near-boiling water and will then set jellies and mousses. Agar-agar gives a slightly softer set than gelatin and jellies made from it will be slightly cloudy rather than crystal clear. A big advantage is that, unlike gelatin, it has no flavour, so you will only taste the other delicious ingredients. Use three tablespoons agar-agar to 600ml/1 pint liquid or see manufacturers' instructions. The following fruit-juice jelly recipe gives the basic method.

FRUIT JUICE JELLIES

600ml/1 pint natural fruit juice
3 tablespoons agar-agar

Put the fruit juice into a saucepan. Sprinkle in the agar-agar. Bring the juice almost to a boil and hold at that temperature for 2–3 minutes, stirring all the time until the agar-agar has dissolved.

Cool the mixture to room temperature. Pour it into a large or several small moulds and put them into the refrigerator for 2 hours for the jelly to set.

RAINBOW JELLIES

Use two or more contrasting colours of fruit juice (such as grape, apple and orange). Make up one colour; pour it in to half fill the moulds. Put it into the refrigerator to set. While the first jelly is setting, make up the second. When it is cold, but not set, pour it onto the first jelly, which should now be set. Return the moulds to the refrigerator for 2 hours.

RASPBERRY MOUSSE

450g/1lb raspberries, fresh or frozen
100g/4oz honey
2 tablespoons water
3 tablespoons agar-agar
2 eggs, separated
150ml/¼ pint double cream

Put the raspberries into a saucepan with the honey and water. Cover and set them on a low heat for 15 minutes or until they are very soft and juicy. Rub them through a sieve, and cool the purée to room temperature.

Reserve 2 tablespoons of the purée. Return the rest to the saucepan and stir in the agar-agar. Bring the purée to just below boiling point and hold at that temperature, stirring, for 2–3 minutes or until the agar-agar has dissolved. Beat in the egg yolks and stir until the mixture thickens, without letting it boil.

Take the pan from the heat and cool the mixture until it is on the point of setting. Lightly whip the cream and stiffly whisk the egg white. Fold first the cream and then the egg white into the raspberry purée.

Pour the mousse into small pots or glasses and leave it in a cool place or in the refrigerator for 2 hours to set. Just before serving, spoon the reserved raspberry purée over the top.

APPLES WITH WALNUT AND APRICOT STUFFING

4 medium cooking apples
100g/4oz shelled walnuts OR almonds OR
**   hazelnuts**
50g/2oz dried whole apricots★
2 tablespoons honey
pinch of ground mace
25g/1oz butter

Heat the oven to 200°C/400°F/Gas 6. Mince together the walnuts and apricots. Mix in the honey and mace. Core the apples and score each one round the centre. Put them onto a buttered, ovenproof dish.

Fill the apples with the nut and fruit mixture. Dot them with butter. Bake the apples for 30 minutes or until tender.

Serve with whipped cream or natural yoghurt.
★Instead of apricots, use dates, raisins or sultanas. If the apricots are replaced with other dried fruits, cinnamon or nutmeg may be used instead of mace.

PEAR FRITTERS WITH APPLE SAUCE

Batter:
100g/4oz wholewheat flour
pinch of salt
1 egg, separated
1 tablespoon oil
150ml/¼ pint milk

Fritters:
4 medium-sized dessert pears, ripe but firm
juice of 1 lemon
2 tablespoons honey, melted

Sauce:
1 tablespoon arrowroot
300ml/½ pint natural apple juice

Garnish:
2 tablespoons hazelnuts, chopped and toasted
   OR other mixed nuts

For the batter, put the flour and salt into a bowl. Make a well in the centre and stir in the egg yolk and oil. Gradually beat in the milk. Let the batter stand for 30 minutes. Just before cooking, stiffly whisk egg white and fold it into the batter.

Peel, quarter and core the pears, and cut each quarter lengthways in half. Lay them in a dish. Pour over the lemon juice and honey. Leave them for 15 minutes.

To make the sauce, put the arrowroot into a bowl and stir in 4 tablespoons of the apple juice. Put the remaining juice into a saucepan and bring it to the boil. Add the arrowroot mixture and stir briskly until the sauce is thick. Remove it from the heat and keep it warm.

To cook, heat a pan of deep oil to 190°C/375°F. Using a skewer or fork, dip the pieces of pear into the batter. Drop them into the oil, four pieces at a time. Fry them until they are golden brown. Lift them onto crumpled kitchen paper to drain. Cook the rest in the same way.

To serve, spoon a little sauce on each of four small plates. Set the pear pieces on top. Sprinkle the nuts round the pieces of pear.

LITTLE POTS OF CAROB AND ORANGE

2 75-g/3-oz orange-flavoured carob bars
juice of ½ large orange
15g/½oz butter or vegetable margarine
3 eggs, separated
chopped walnuts for garnish, optional

Break up the carob bars and put them into a saucepan
with the orange juice. Set them on a low heat and stir
continuously with a wooden spoon until the carob
has melted and you have a smooth, creamy mixture.
Quickly beat in the butter or margarine.

Take the pan from the heat and beat in the egg
yolks, one at a time, while the mixture is still hot.
Whip the egg whites to a firm snow and stir them
briskly into the carob mixture.

Pour the mixture into small pots such as ramekins,
individual soufflé dishes or small, round chocolate
pots. Put them into the refrigerator for 4 hours for the
carob mixture to set. It will not become as firm and
set as a mousse but is more like a very thick, fluffy
custard.

Sprinkle the chopped walnuts over the top before
serving, if wished.

HOT SPICED APPLE CAKE

2 large cooking apples
100g/4oz butter or vegetable margarine plus
    extra for greasing
75g/3oz Barbados sugar
2 eggs, beaten
4 tablespoons apple juice or sweet sherry
225g/8oz wholewheat flour
1 teaspoon bicarbonate of soda
1 teaspoon cinnamon
freshly grated nutmeg (about ¼ nut) OR ¼
    teaspoon ground nutmeg
50g/2oz currants
75g/3oz raisins

Heat the oven to 170°C/325°F/Gas 3. Peel, core and
finely chop the apples. Cream the butter or margarine in a mixing bowl and beat in the sugar. Beat in
the eggs and then the apple juice or sherry, a little at a
time.

Toss the flour with the bicarbonate of soda and
spices. Beat it into the butter, sugar and eggs. Mix in
the apples and dried fruits.

Put the mixture into a well-greased 20-cm/8-in
diameter 4–5-cm/1½–2-inch deep, ovenproof dish.
Bake it for 1½ hours or until a skewer inserted in the
centre comes out clean.

Serve hot directly from the dish and hand whipped
cream, single cream, soured cream or natural
yoghurt separately.

CHERRY PUDDING

100g/4oz stoned dates
50g/2oz dried apple rings
150ml/¼ pint apple juice
175g/6oz wholewheat flour
1 teaspoon bicarbonate of soda
3 eggs, beaten
6 tablespoons corn oil plus extra for greasing
One 400-g/14-oz tin stoned black cherries
6 tablespoons sugar-free jam, preferably red-coloured

Finely chop the dates and apple rings. Put them into a bowl and pour in the apple juice. Leave them to soak for at least 4 hours. Liquidise the fruits with the juice.

Heat the oven to 350°F/180°C/Gas 4. Put the flour and bicarbonate of soda into a bowl. Make a well in the centre. Put in the liquidised fruits, eggs and corn oil. Gradually beat in the flour from the sides of the well until you have a smooth, thick batter.

Drain the cherries, discarding the juice. Put them into an oiled 20-cm/8-in diameter soufflé dish (or other deep ovenproof dish). Cover them with the jam. Put in the pudding mixture. Bake the pudding for 45 minutes or until browned and risen and a skewer stuck in the centre comes out clean. Serve straight from the dish.

BAKEWELL TART

Shortcrust pastry made with 175g/6oz wholewheat flour, 75g/3oz margarine (p.50, adapted)
50g/2oz dried whole apricots
150ml/¼ pint natural orange juice
4 tablespoons apricot jam, sugar-free if possible
40g/1½oz wholewheat cake crumbs (see sponge cake p.53)
50g/2oz ground almonds
1 egg, beaten
grated rind and juice of ½ lemon

Put the apricots into a saucepan with the orange juice. Bring them to the boil. Remove them from the heat and soak them for 4 hours. Drain the apricots and then liquidise them with 4 tablespoons of the juice.

Heat the oven to 180°C/350°F/Gas 4. Roll out the pastry and use it to line a 20-cm/8-in tart tin. Spread it with the apricot jam.

Mix together the liquidised apricots, cake crumbs, almonds, egg and lemon rind and juice. Spread the mixture over the jam.

Bake the tart for 40 minutes or until the filling is set and browned. Serve warm.

RHUBARB AND SULTANA PIE

Pastry:
225g/8oz wholewheat flour
pinch of salt
1 teaspoon bicarbonate of soda
100g/4oz butter or vegetable margarine
4 tablespoons cold water
beaten egg for glaze

Filling:
450g/1lb rhubarb
100ml/3½ fl oz red grape juice
50g/2oz sultanas
75g/3oz honey
2 tablespoons tapioca OR sago

Put the flour, salt and soda into a bowl. Rub in the butter or margarine. Mix to a dough with the water. Leave the pastry in a cool place.

Chop the rhubarb and put it into a saucepan with the grape juice, sultanas and honey. Bring them to the boil; cover and simmer for 15 minutes so that the rhubarb is soft.

Take the pan from the heat and stir in the tapioca or sago. Leave until the rhubarb is completely cold.

Heat the oven to 200°C/400°F/Gas 6. Roll out about two-thirds of the pastry and use it to line an 18-cm/7-in diameter, 2.5-cm/1-in deep pie plate. Put in the rhubarb mixture and cover it with the remaining pastry. Seal edges and brush top with beaten egg.

Bake the pie for 35 minutes or until the top is golden brown.

Serve the pie hot with single cream or yoghurt, or cold with whipped cream.

Dishes for vegetarian entertaining can be just as special as those that include meat or fish. The many delicious and exotic ingredients for you to choose from do justice to any table. Think of globe artichokes, avocados or cashew nuts, for example.

Even everyday ingredients, such as chickpeas or rice, can be transformed into a meal fit for a king if you add spices and other flavourful ingredients, and if you take special care to make them into dishes that you would not normally consider for a family meal.

Think, too, of your presentation. That tiny sprig of parsley, that strip of bright tomato, or the shape into which you make your nut patties can make all the difference between a good meal and one that is absolutely perfect.

MENU 1.

Cucumber stuffed with Cheese and Mint
Chickpea and Apricot Curry
Vegetable Curry
Plain brown rice (p.40)
Spiced Pineapple

CUCUMBER STUFFED WITH CHEESE AND MINT

1 small cucumber
100g/4oz curd cheese
1 tablespoon chopped mint
1 clove garlic, crushed
juice of ½ lemon
freshly ground black pepper
mint leaves or parsley sprigs
4 small tomatoes

Cut the cucumber in half lengthways and scoop out all the seeds. Put the cheese into a bowl and mix in the mint, garlic, lemon juice and pepper. Pack the mixture into the hollows in the cucumbers and sandwich the two halves together.

Cut the cucumber into 1-cm/½-in thick slices. Put them onto a flat plate and chill them for 15 minutes.

Cut the tomatoes into thin wedges. Put the cucumber slices onto four small serving plates. Garnish each one with a mint leaf or parsley sprig and arrange tomato wedges between them.

CHICKPEA AND APRICOT CURRY

225g/8oz chickpeas
75g/3oz dried whole apricots
200ml/7 fl oz natural orange juice
4 tablespoons oil
2 medium onions, thinly sliced
1 garlic clove, finely chopped
2 teaspoons ground cumin
2 teaspoons curry powder
1 teaspoon paprika
300ml/½ pint Basic vegetable stock (p.6)

Either soak the chickpeas overnight; or put them into a saucepan, bring them to the boil, boil them for 2 minutes, take the pan from the heat and leave the chickpeas in the water for 2 hours. Drain the chickpeas. Put them into a saucepan with fresh water. Bring them to the boil and boil them for 10 minutes. Then cover and simmer for 2–3 hours or until they are soft. Drain them.

Soak the apricots in the orange juice for 4 hours. Drain them and cut them into thin strips.

Heat the oil in a saucepan on a low heat. Put in the onions and garlic and cook them until they are golden. Add the cumin, curry powder and paprika; cook, stirring, for 2 minutes. Pour in the stock and bring it to the boil. Put in the chickpeas and apricots; cover and simmer for 30 minutes.

VEGETABLE CURRY

1 medium cauliflower
225g/8oz carrots
2 medium courgettes
2 green peppers
2 medium onions
4 green chilli
3 tablespoons oil
2 cloves garlic, finely chopped
25g/1oz fresh ginger root, peeled and grated
2 teaspoons curry powder
1 teaspoon turmeric
1 teaspoon cumin seeds
75g/3oz creamed coconut, chopped★
150ml/¼ pint Basic vegetable stock (p.6)

Cut the cauliflower into small florettes. Thinly slice the carrots and courgettes. Core and deseed the peppers and cut them into 2.5-cm/1-in strips. Thinly slice the onions. Core, deseed and finely chop the chilli.

Heat the oil in a saucepan over a low heat. Mix in the onion, garlic, chilli and ginger and cook them until the onions are soft. Stir in the curry powder, turmeric and cumin seeds; cook for 1 minute more. Put in the coconut and stir until it melts. Fold in the vegetables. Pour in the stock and bring to the boil. Cover and cook on a moderate heat for 20 minutes.
★ *Creamed coconut* comes in the form of a hard white block. It can be bought in 200g/7oz packets from most supermarkets and health shops.

SPICED PINEAPPLE

2 medium pineapples
150ml/¼ pint pineapple juice
2 tablespoons honey
4 cardamom pods, bruised
4 pieces preserved stem ginger, finely chopped
3 tablespoons flaked almonds, toasted

Cut the husk from the pineapples. Cut the flesh into 1-cm/½-in thick slices. Remove the cores using an apple corer, or knife. Lay the rings, overlapping slightly, into a flat ovenproof dish. (Use two dishes if necessary.)

Put the pineapple juice, honey and cardamom pods into a small pan. Heat them on a low heat, without boiling, for 15 minutes. Strain the juice and pour it over the pineapple rings.

Heat the grill to high. Place the dishes of pineapple under the grill for about 5 minutes or until the pineapple has heated through and is just beginning to brown. Scatter the pineapple with the ginger and almonds flakes.

MENU 2

Eggs with Avocado Sauce
Brazil Nut Hearts with Tomato and Soured
Cream Sauce
Stir-Fried Spiced Cabbage
Ginger Ice Cream

EGGS WITH AVOCADO SAUCE

4 eggs, hard-boiled
1 ripe avocado
3 tablespoons natural yoghurt
½ tablespoons tomato purée
¼ teaspoon Tabasco sauce
4 tablespoons chopped parsley
8 large lettuce leaves
2 boxes mustard and cress
1 large tomato

Cut the eggs in half lengthways. Halve, stone and peel the avocado. Mash it to a smooth paste and mix in the yoghurt, tomato purée, Tabasco and parsley.

Put two lettuce leaves on each of four small plates and arrange the cress in a circle on top of the leaves. Put the egg halves in the centre, cut side down. Spoon the avocado sauce over the top.

Scald, peel and deseed the tomato. Cut it into thin strips. Garnish each egg with a strip of tomato.

BRAZIL NUT HEARTS WITH TOMATO AND SOURED CREAM SAUCE

175g/6oz brazil nuts
175g/6oz wholewheat bread
2 tablespoons oil
1 large onion, finely chopped
100g/4oz split red lentils
450ml/¾ pint Basic vegetable stock (p.6)
1 tablespoon chopped thyme
1 tablespoon chopped marjoram
4 sage leaves, chopped
4 tablespoons chopped parsley
2 tablespoons tomato purée
50g/2oz wholewheat flour
1 egg, beaten
oil for deep frying
8 small parsley sprigs

Sauce:
450g/1lb tomatoes
1 small onion
bouquet garni
4 tablespoons Basic vegetable stock (p.6)
150ml/¼ pint soured cream

Finely chop or grind the brazil nuts. Make the bread into crumbs. Heat the oil in a saucepan over a low heat. Put in the onion and soften it. Stir in the lentils

and cook for 1 minute. Pour in the stock and bring it to the boil. Add the thyme, marjoram and sage. Cover and simmer for 30 minutes or until the lentils are very soft.

Take the pan from the heat. Mix in the brazil nuts and fresh breadcrumbs. Leave the mixture until it is quite cold.

To make the sauce, chop the tomatoes and onion. Put them into a saucepan with the bouquet garni and stock. Bring them to the boil. Cover and simmer for 30 minutes or until the tomatoes are very soft. Remove the bouquet garni. Put the tomatoes and onion through a vegetable mill or rub them through an ordinary sieve. Return the purée to the cleaned pan. Simmer, uncovered, for 20 minutes or until the purée has thickened and reduced by about one-third. Take the pan from the heat and stir in the soured cream.

Mix the parsley into the brazil nut mixture. Make the mixture into small hearts, using a biscuit cutter as a mould. Coat the shapes in flour, then in the beaten egg and then in more flour.

Bring a pan of deep oil to 190°C/375°F. Deep fry the hearts until they are golden brown. To serve, put a pool of sauce on each of four dinner plates. Set the hearts on top and garnish each with a parsley sprig. Serve any remaining sauce separately.

STIR-FRIED SPICED CABBAGE

1 large green cabbage
4 tablespoons oil
1 clove garlic, finely chopped
2 teaspoons paprika
1 teaspoon turmeric
¼ teaspoon cayenne

Finely shred the cabbage. Heat the oil in a wok, or very large frying pan over a high heat. Put in the cabbage and stir for about 4 minutes or until it begins to wilt.

Lower the heat and add the spices. Continue stirring for a further 3–4 minutes or until the cabbage is just tender.

GINGER ICE CREAM

300ml/½ pint double cream
300ml/½ pint natural yoghurt
3 tablespoons syrup from the ginger jar
pinch of fine sea salt
6 pieces preserved stem ginger, finely chopped

Whip the cream until it is slightly thickened. Whip in the yoghurt so the mixture becomes light and fluffy. Whip in the ginger syrup and salt and fold in the chopped ginger.

Put the mixture into a bowl or freezing tray and put it into the coldest part of the freezer or the freezing compartment of the refrigerator (at the lowest setting). Freeze it until it is slushy, about 2 hours.

Take the mixture out and whip it again so it becomes fluffy and smooth. Freeze it for a further 4 hours. Either take out the ice cream, leave it for 30 minutes at room temperature and serve; or whip it again and put it into a plastic container for storing. It will keep in the freezing compartment of the refrigerator for up to two weeks and in the freezer for up to three months.

INDEX

Agar-agar 54
Almond:
  Red cabbage and almonds in cider 23
Apple:
  Apples with walnut and apricot
    stuffing 55
  Hot spiced apple cake 57
  Spiced apple rice 41
Apricot, almond and cherry cakes 52
Aubergine:
  French bread filled with spiced
    aubergines 26
  Grilled aubergines with sesame seeds 10
  Spiced aubergine and courgette kebabs 39
Avocado:
  Eggs with avocado sauce 62
  Avocado with green pepper cheese 12
  Avocado omelette 20
  Baked potatoes topped with avocado 29

Bakewell tart 58
Barley 40; bake with carrots 42
Bean:
  French bread filled with beans and
    corn 27
  Leek and bean macaroni 18
  Pinto beans with millet and cheese 15
  Spiced black-eyed bean and rice soup 15
  Two-bean simmer pot 14
Bean sprout and mushroom salad 37
Brazil nut hearts with tomato and soured
  cream sauce 62
Brioches, nut-filled 49
Brown rice 40
Brussels sprouts with black olives 33
Buckwheat 40
Burghul wheat 40:
  Burghul, celery and nut salad 28
  Burghul and green olive salad 42
  Curried wheat and lentil loaf 19

Cabbage. See also Red cabbage
  Cabbage with apple and green
    peppers 38
  Cabbage, grape and raisin salad 36
  Curried Savoy with cashews and
    eggs 22
  Hearty cabbage omelette 18
  Stir-fried spiced cabbage 63
Carob cake, wholewheat 53
Carob and orange, little pots of 57
Carrot:
  Baked julienne of carrots and onions 32
  Barley bake with carrots 42
  Carrot and banana salad 12
  Carrot and walnut quiche 50
  Grated carrot soup 7
Cauliflower soup with cheese 7
Celery and apple soup, curried 8
Celery, radish and apple salad 36
Celery and walnut salad, hot 11

Cheese:
  Cheese pastry 51
  Cheese, potato and corn bake 31
  Cheesy scone whirls 47
  Feta cheese salad 25
  Mushroom and mozzarella risotto 25
  Tagliatelle with beetroot and cheese
    sauce 24
  Tomato macaroni cheese 24
  Tomatoes full of Camembert 11
Cherry pudding 58
Chickpea and apricot curry 61
Chickpea, celery and apple salad 16
Chicory, grape and orange salad 13
Courgette:
  Spaghetti with courgettes and
    walnuts 30
  Spiced aubergine and courgette
    kebabs 39
Cucumber and blue cheese salad 38
Cucumber stuffed with cheese and
  mint 60
Curried dishes:
  Curried celery and apple soup 8
  Curried millet with mushrooms 43
  Curried Savoy with cashews and
    eggs 22
  Curried wheat and lentil loaf 19
  Chickpea and apricot curry 61
  Vegetable curry 61

Date and peanut tea bread 52

Egg:
  Avocado omelette 20
  Curried Savoy with cashews and
    eggs 22
  Eggs with avocado sauce 62
  Green pea and tomato scramble 30
  Hearty cabbage omelette 18
  Pasta and spinach scramble 20

Feta cheese salad 25
French bread filled with beans and
  corn 27; filled with spiced
  aubergines 26
French dressing 34
Fruit juice jellies 54

Ginger ice cream 63
Green pea and tomato scramble 30

Kasha 40; with celery and yoghurt 43

Leek and bean macaroni 18
Leek, carrot and potato soup 8
Leek roulade 21
Lentil:
  Brown lentils with parsley and
    watercress 16
  Curried wheat and lentil loaf 19
  Green lentil ratatouille 17

Macaroni:
  Leek and bean macaroni 18
  Tomato macaroni cheese 24
Mayonnaise 35
Millet 40; curried, with mushrooms 43
Mushroom and mozzarella risotto 25
Mushroom pizza, scone-based 46

Nuts. See also Almond, Walnut
  Burghul, celery and nut salad 28
  Nut-filled brioches 49
  Polenta with nuts and tomatoes 23
  Tomatoes baked with mixed nuts 39

Onion, mushroom and green pepper
  soup 9
Onions with orange stuffing 32

Pasta with peas and curd cheese 45
Pasta and spinach scramble 20
Pear fritters with apple sauce 56
Pepper:
  Avocado with green pepper cheese 12
  Cabbage with apple and green
    peppers 38
  Mixed pepper tart 51
  Tomato and red pepper salad 37
Pineapple, spiced 61
Pizza, scone-based mushroom 46
Polenta 40, 44; with nuts and tomatoes 23;
  with onions and tomatoes 44
Potato:
  Baked potatoes topped with avocado 29
  Cheese, potato and corn bake 31
  Jacket potatoes with soured cream
    and dill 33

Rainbow jellies 54
Raspberry mousse 55
Red cabbage and almonds in cider 23
Rhubarb and sultana pie 59
Rice:
  Brown rice with parsley and lemon 40
  Rice and red pepper salad 41
  Spiced apple rice 41

Scone-based mushroom pizza 46
Scone whirls, cheesy 47
Shortcrust pastry 50
Spaghetti with courgettes and walnuts 30;
  with mixed vegetable sauce 45
Stock 6

Tagliatelle with beetroot and cheese sauce
  24
Tomato:
  Simple tomato soup 9
  Tomato, bread and sunflower salad 28
  Tomato macaroni cheese 24
  Tomato and red pepper salad 37
  Tomatoes baked with mixed nuts 39
  Tomatoes full of Camembert 11
Two-bean simmer pot 14

Vegetable:
  Basic vegetable stock 6
  Spaghetti with mixed vegetable sauce 45
  Vegetable curry 61

Walnut:
  Apples with walnut and apricot
    stuffing 55
  Carrot and walnut quiche 50
  Hot celery and walnut salad 11
Wholewheat bread 48
Wholewheat sponge cake 53

Yoghurt dressings and mayonnaise 35